MASS PERSUASION IN HISTORY

Frontispiece: The Statue of Liberty, New York; a gift from the French to the American people

Mass Persuasion
in History

An Historical Analysis of the Development
of Propaganda Techniques

Oliver Thomson

Crane, Russak & Company, Inc.
New York

This Edition published 1977 by
Crane, Russak & Company, Inc., New York,
by arrangement with
Paul Harris Publishing, Edinburgh

ISBN 0 - 8448 - 1076 - 2

Library of Congress Catalog Card No. 76 - 52881

Printed in Scotland by the Shetland Times Ltd.,
Lerwick, Shetland.

"It would be dangerous to assume that the power of a modern national community to mould the character and thought of its individual members and to produce a certain degree of conformity and uniformity among them is any less than that of a primitive tribe."

—*E. H. Carr.*

CONTENTS

PART I — THE VOCABULARY OF LEADERSHIP

INTRODUCTION - - - - - - - - 3
EVIDENCE AND SOURCES - - - - - - - 8
TYPOLOGY - - - - - - - - - 11
    Objectives - - - - - - - - 11
    Media - - - - - - - - - 13
    Message - - - - - - - - - 15
    Inhibiting Factors - - - - - - - 23
    Intensifying Factors - - - - - - 26
    Side Effects - - - - - - - - 28
CRITERIA OF PENETRATION - - - - - - 30
AUDIENCE ANALYSIS - - - - - - - 31
RESPONSE ANALYSIS - - - - - - - 32
ACCESS TO MEDIA - - - - - - - - 36
MEDIA DEVELOPMENT - - - - - - - 39

PART II — HISTORICAL CASE STUDIES

THE ROMAN EMPIRE - - - - - - - 55
THE PAPACY - - - - - - - - 67
THE REFORMATION - - - - - - - - 75
THE REVOLUTIONARY PERIOD - - - - - - 82
NINETEENTH CENTURY PROPAGANDA - - - - 98
LENIN AND COMMUNISM - - - - - - - 104
HITLER AND FASCISM - - - - - - - 111
MODERN CHINA - - - - - - - - 119
DEMOCRACY AND THE WESTERN WORLD - - - - 124
EPILOGUE - - - - - - - - - 119
BIBLIOGRAPHY - - - - - - - - - 133
INDEX - - - - - - - - - - 139

ILLUSTRATIONS

ARCHITECTURE AND SCULPTURE

Frontispiece: The Statue of Liberty, New York; a gift from the French to the American people

1 Reconstruction of Aztec temples in Mexico: a remarkable early example of cybernetic architecture
2 Monument to the Soviet Cosmonauts, Moscow
3 Russian Communist use of sculpture; stainless steel statue in Moscow
4 The column of Marcius Aurelius in Rome, with its strip-history propaganda message from top to bottom
5 The Chrysler Building, New York: architecture as a success symbol
6 Moscow Exhibition of Achievements
7 Entrance to Exhibition of Achievements, Moscow

ANCILLARY MEDIA

8 One of Julius Caesar's coins: the first genuine mass medium for political propaganda in history
9 A tobacco jar used to help to promote the French Revolution
10 Playing cards, a popular propaganda medium in the sixteenth to eighteenth centuries
11 Commemorative medal helping to boost the image of John Paul Jones
12 Jacobin medals showing French understanding of need to repeat visual symbols

SYMBOLS AND RITUALS

13 The standards of Roman Imperial Legions in the first century A.D.
14 The cumulative effect of massed swastikas in 1934
15 U.S. Democratic Party Rally
16 A ceremony of the new Republican Religion of Reason in Notre Dame, Paris 1793
17 British Imperial ritual: Victoria proclaimed Empress of India, 1867
18 Typical Nazi ritual, 1935

MUSIC

19 Music for motivation: the song book of the Prussian Grenadiers in 1756
20 The hit song of 1792: *The Marseillaise*

ILLUSTRATION

21 An early stage in the creation of Napoleon's image; the dashing commander

22 Napoleon's image moves a stage further towards apotheosis

23 Dürer's *Four Horsemen of the Apocalypse,* typical of the millennial promotions of the early fifteenth century

24 The Catholics use caricature in the battle against Luther

25 Hong Kong Family Planning poster copied from similar Brititsh theme.

26 Indian projection of ideal family size

27 *The Fall of the Bastille;* the visual oversimplification of the French Revolution

28 The martyrdom of Boston turned into pictorial legend by Paul Revere

29 *Der Sturmer:* a typical front page in 1935: note long anti-semitic poem with reference to Dachau

POSTERS

30 A British war poster of 1944 modelled on the famous Kitchener 'YOUR Country needs YOU'

31 Nazi anti-semitic poster

32 and 33 The British Labour Party General Election Campaign of 1963

34 The Red Parade in Peking; Poster 1965

35 The peasants applaud Chairman Mao; Poster 1965

FILM

36 and 37 Stills from Nazi propaganda film *Swastika*

38 and 39 Still from Kinopravda news bulletin on the death of Lenin

ACKNOWLEDGEMENTS

Mexican Institute of Anthropology and Archaeology, 1

Imperial War Museum, London, 29, 31

Radio Times Hulton Picture Library, Frontispiece, 5

Mary Evans Picture Library, London, 9, 10, 11, 12, 14, 16, 17, 18, 19, 20, 21, 22, 23, 24, 27, 28, 30, 34, 35 and dust jacket

British Film Institute, London, 36, 37, 38, 39

The Labour Party, Transport House, London, 32, 33

Paul Harris, 2, 3, 6, 7

Associated Press, 15, 25, 26

PART ONE

THE VOCABULARY OF LEADERSHIP

INTRODUCTION

Throughout history, communication, even if it was only the communication of violence, has been one of the major components of leadership. Yet planned or target communications, the cybernetic techniques employed by one ruling group after another, have received, until recently, remarkably little attention from historians. Only since writers such as McLuhan began to point out that 'the products of self-knowledge were being kidnapped and put to work in the service of deliberate control', has there been any real interest in the influence of media and messages. Even that tends to imply that mass persuasion is some new monster of the twentieth century.

It is the object of this study to examine the development of mass persuasion techniques since the time of the Roman Empire, and to try to review, if only briefly, the cybernetic skills used both by establishments and rebels, both in the political and religious fields. It tries to offer a means of comparing the development of media, the techniques used to exploit them, the styles and themes which have proved effective during different periods of history; in other words, it tries to analyse the influences of and trends in what Barthes called 'the myriad rites of communciation which rule social appearances'.

The word used in everyday language to describe the manipulation of media for social control is propaganda. This word was coined in the sixteenth century when Roman Catholicism took a new look at its communications in the face of attacks by the Protestants. Since then, most governments have been coy about using the word and its associations have been bad. For the time being, it is important to reserve any moral judgements and instead to recognise the breadth of activity which the propaganda concept truly covers. Lasswell, the American pioneer of propaganda studies, defined it variously as 'the manipulation of public opinion by means of political symbols' or, 'the management of collective attitudes by the manipulation of significant symbols'. On another occasion he differentiated between education which was 'the passing on of accepted skills' and propaganda, 'the passing on of controversial attitudes'. This, in fact, recalls the age-old ideological split between Socrates and his fellow Greek philosophers. While Socrates pursued the dream of absolute truth, his rivals felt that this was impracticable and recommended that, for the sake of civic harmony, certain public attitudes should be cultivated. Plato advised such a propaganda structure in his *Republic,* using the word 'lie', and helping to perpetuate the concept of propaganda as a black art and as the opposite of truthful information. But the distinction is misleading. In reality, it is hard to find any piece of communication which is totally devoid of propaganda content or intention. As H. J. Gans put it, 'no novel or play is impartial'. Neither is any piece of music, graphic art, poetry, history or any other form of message. Excessive differentiation between transmitting information for non-cybernetic purposes and transmitting propaganda messages, is often hypocritical. It is like the missionary saying 'I teach God's truth and all else is propaganda'. Hoggart is one of a number of recent British writers who have attacked the idea of propaganda; he describes 'advertising, propaganda, and most religious proselytising, and any other form of emotional blackmail . . . , the exploitation of human inadequacy. Similarly, Vance Packard frightened half a generation of Americans with his somewhat naïve horror at what he thought were the novel methods of political merchandising practised in the USA after the introduction of television. 'The manipulation of the people by a tyrant with a controlled society is now a fairly simple matter', he wrote. We must question both the novelty and the simplicity. The distinction between true and false or the truthful use of false information or the false use of true information becomes largely meaningless.

Propaganda is a wide-ranging subject, one on which people hold strong views, yet which is little understood. McLuhan, as ever, desribes it most evocatively when he tells how a new message system 'dunks the entire population in a new imagery'. Similarly Gerbner talks of 'the cultivation of dominant image patterns as the major function of the dominant communication agency in any society'. In other words, a historical review of propaganda techniques and social control must not just cover the more obvious forms, but the entire message system or semiology of a society or period; every symbol, every ritual, every work of art, every crude cliché.

The relevance of this study should be clarified from the point of view of three different disciplines: history, communicology and ethics.

History is often a tired subject, rewritten regularly not just in the light of new source material, but often because new sciences or disciplines have been applied to it, or simply because of changes in outlook or fashion.

Regrettably, from the point of view of cybernetics little research has been done. Although success or failure in image projection can be seen readily enough as one of the most important single factors in the success or failure of a political or religious movement, there have been to date very few studies of propaganda in a historical setting. Even when propaganda is mentioned, as it often is, in studies of Napoleon or Lenin, Caesar or Hitler, the treatment is usually cursory. Toynbee in his great, *Study of History,* refers to mimesis and social drill as a means of propaganda, but makes no attempt to explain how it worked. In many periods such as the Crusades, the Reformation, the Second British Empire, propaganda is almost totally ignored. For that reason, it seems justifiable to make at least an attempt to tie together the various components of the propoganda story, and to see what contribution this makes to our understanding of certain crucial periods of history.

Communicology itself is a very young discipline. Although Plato in his *Republic* showed such a remarkable feeling for the power of propaganda, and although Aristotle's *Rhetoric* contains a brilliant analysis of oral communication, the study of media usage was largely ignored until in the twentieth century mass media and mass dictatorships forced sociologists to take propaganda seriously. The classic work of Lasswell in the late thirties led to a number of other American studies of propaganda methods. The Second World War encouraged a new and much more sophisticated approach to propaganda techniques and led to empirical research projects with controlled population samples. Worry about the social effects of mass media and the desire to make party political campaigns more sophisticated have also inspired much research in Europe. Although much work remains to be done, particularly on deeper and longer-term aspects of attitude change by means of propaganda, it still seems reasonable to look away for a while from today's controlled experiments, and see if any deductions can be drawn from a review of some of yesterday's massive, often haphazard and ill-recorded propaganda campaigns.

The ethical point of view on propaganda is one that easily causes controversy and invites snap judgements. It is proposed in this study to examine the techniques adopted by individuals or groups, consciously or unconsciously, to help lead, cajole, rule, govern, subjugate, convert or influence other groups. As we have seen, it is easy to become alarmist and to condemn all forms of propaganda, without appreciating 'the myriad small rites' which help societies to function.

There is a need to find some guidelines for a balanced judgement on the use of media and communication techniques for achieving acceptable levels of social indoctrination in a democratic society. While the American public relations concept of 'the engineering of consent' may seem distasteful, we have to realise that the total rejection of propaganda is anarchic; unless by propaganda we mean only those aspects of communication which are against our point of view. From a humanistic standpoint, there may be some standard by which techniques of social control and education can be justified on the grounds of increasing human happiness, eliminating war, reducing population growth, encouraging hygiene and so on. Perhaps, also we may even find some room for tolerating an element of 'enthusiasm'. This is the kind of the special communication which man propagandises yet feels to have come from a source beyond himself. In other words there may be ends, many of them, which justify the means of, to quote Hoggart again, 'exploiting human inadequacies, by means of political or religious propaganda. We shall see too that many of the premises of democracy come into question in this context. We come up against the concepts of majority tyranny and minority acquiescence.

There is the blurred and unacceptable distinction, in much contemporary writing, between communicating facts and projecting ideas or attitudes. As Williams puts it 'the basic purpose of communication, the sharing of human experience can become subordinated to the drive to sell something'. One questions whether there is not always an unbreakable link between the two. For example, Kaarle Nordenstreng argues 'news should consist of the systematic explication of the ultimate goals of society'. But let us appreciate that there is, at best, only a marginal moral superiority of democratically selected goals over those which might be promoted by a commercial, political or religious dictator. It should also be appreciated that, in so far as the distinction between the persuasive and non-persuasive elements in communication can be so blurred, then the education of populations to appreciate the difference, can be put forward as a useful form of prophylaxis against misused propaganda.

Sweeping ethical condemnations of propaganda are therefore dangerous, and perhaps eventually we may be able to offer tentative criteria for making moral judgements on propaganda as a whole or on particular examples. Similarly, a degree of hesitation is advisable even in suggesting pointers to the technical improvement of propaganda for good causes, because of the dangers of abuse. But such hesitation is a good deal less relevant than increasing our understanding of propaganda so that we are better able to be selective about the messages we accept.

At this stage it is also important to define in greater depth what is meant by propaganda. It includes any means of projecting or transmitting images, ideas, or information which influences behaviour in an active or passive sense. This covers almost every aspect of art and communication, because nearly all messages have either deliberately or accidentally some persuasive content. Lasswell does draw a distinction between planned propaganda and the unpremeditated contagion of ideas. But this distinction could be very confusing, because often much real propaganda is passed on subconsciously by dedicated devotees of a cause. As Gans put it, each group of society 'tries to get its own particular values legitimated by the media and they affect the distribution of power, wealth and prestige by controlling the symbols, myths and information'.

Another distinction which does have greater validity is that drawn between agitation and propaganda. Lenin drew attention to this, particularly when he opted for a programme of converting the elite instead of direct mass propaganda. But propaganda is not the same as force. Direct terrorisation of populations or brainwashing on their own rarely create genuine changes of attitude. Propaganda techniques may exploit credulity, twist ideas or play on emotions, but they do not include the application of brute strength or straight threats. While it will be seen that an element of force or agitation is often associated with propaganda, it is not part of it and usually indicates a weakness on the part of the propagandist or his message.

B

EVIDENCE AND SOURCES

It is only fair to admit at the outset of this study that the historical evidence is often inadequate. Sources on the circulation, penetration and effects of propaganda are very limited. Even for the most recent periods of history statistics on media are unreliable. Attempts can be made to calculate roughly the number of times the average Roman saw his emperor's face on coins, statues, or pictures; or how often and in how many different forms the medieval peasant saw the cross each day. But retrospective statistics are even less reliable than the modern variety. Even population and literacy figures are too limited to allow for more than guesses about media penetration. Similarly while there are often edition or circulation figures for pamphlets and newspapers in the early stages of printing, readership per copy in the eras of Wilkes or Marat is much harder to quantify, particularly when you include coffee shop readership or the effects of reading aloud to groups. Even in the twentieth century figures for multiple media penetration are difficult to come by and our evaluation of propaganda campaigns as recent as those of Hitler and Stalin must to some extent be guesswork. Nevertheless a number of useful conclusions about past propaganda campaigns can be drawn even without accurate statistics. For instance, what survives in large quantities is the message material itself, and evidence about the influence it had. We can still sit in a medieval cathedral, absorb the stained glass, images, music and general atmosphere in a way which helps us to understand the massive dominance of the church over attitude formation in the Middle Ages. With other messages, it is sometimes harder to relive the reaction of original audiences. The New Testament, for instance, once a simple document, now requires scholarly explanations, whilst the imagery of many great propaganda poems, tunes and pictures is lost on a modern audience. Certain media and styles are, by their very nature, transient; music, posters, especially those of the painted or graffiti type, tend to disappear or lose their meaning. What can be done, however, is to re-examine the standard historical texts in the light of our new improved appreciation of media usage, and try to place in perspective such evidence of cybernetic skill as we find, period by period. At the same time we can take advantage of some of the methodologies developed for the analysis of contemporary propaganda. There are four areas where this can be deployed: content analysis, attitudinal surveys, persuasion psychology and statistical media analysis.

Content analysis, word by word or sentence by sentence, is now a fairly well developed technique. At its most basic, it can quantify the percentage ratio of for example, fair-haired, blue-eyed heroes, to dark swarthy villains in a novel and draw appropriate conclusions. At this level, it is only a very superficial aid in the study of factors leading to attitudinal change. On the other hand, content analysis by theme, style and techniques is very much in its infancy and naturally it is much more difficult to quantify abstract ideas than individual words or phrases. In a historical context, therefore, the most that can be done at this stage is to draw attention to the more obvious pattern frequencies that come from a general view of contents. This at least makes possible a broad understanding of the way in which certain themes and styles recur in different situations and of the way in which similar results were achieved.

The second area to be examined is that of attitudinal surveys, a commonplace of modern politics and modern marketing, in which on a wide variety of issues the public are questioned about their views. To conduct such surveys retrospectively is clearly a scientific impossibility; even the results of the most recent Gallup or opinion polls are often viewed with a good deal of cynicism. They can contain psychological or statistical biases which cast a shadow over their credibility. But at least we are, historically speaking, in some position to observe results. We may not know precisely how many people were influenced by Buddha or St Paul or Lenin, but we know that large numbers were, and that the attitudinal change was considerable. Persuasion psychology is a difficult area. While there are frequent attempts to re-examine particular historical episodes or personalities in the light of Freudian or Pavlovian psychology, there is as yet no definitive and all embracing theory of persuasion which can allow for a methodical analysis of each act of political or religious conversion. There are partially conflicting and partially overlapping theories of suggestion, imitation, contagion, illusion and delusion. These are applied to instincts, habits, situations, attitudes and responses. As historians, we can be eclectic and make use of those theories which have practical applications. The precise biological or neurological mechanisms do not particularly concern us; rather the broad, accepted traits of human nature which the propagandist may consciously or unconsciously exploit. It is possible to observe different levels of reception and retention of propaganda messages which we can show to have been achieved at various periods in the past using various different components from the propaganda toolbox. We can accept the idea of residual imagery as the foundation of most propaganda, acknowledging that long-term creation of attitudes is usually more significant than short-term conversion attempts.

The other methodology which has some historical applications is media research; the analysis of circulation figures, readership, opportunities to see or hear, and penetration figures. Even in contemporary use these figures have their limitations, since opportunities to see, do not equal, indeed cannot even be correlated to, actual reception, let alone the retention of messages. Similarly, while there are some semi-reliable circulation or edition figures — for instance by knowing the number of editions of each of Luther's works, the average number of copies per edition and the total number of his works — Dickens has estimated that around 300,000 books or pamphlets by Luther were published in ten years. It is still almost impossible to estimate readership retrospectively and there are many important periods where even basic statistics are almost entirely absent. For example, there are a number of significant missing circulation figures in the stories both of the French and Russian revolutions. Nevertheless, in most historical situations it is possible to arrive at some kind of reasonable guess at the general penetration of the main media of that particular period or society. At least the approximate level of exposure of the population to the mainstream propaganda themes can be arrived at, sufficient for us to make some evaluation of the overall effectiveness, grasp of technique and general implications of cybernetic efficiency. Combined with such records as we have of attitudinal change and content analysis of surviving message material, the episode can be placed in its historical context in the general development of propaganda technique. We can also speculate about the duplication of rival media in a society. For instance how many Frenchmen in the thirteenth century both saw stained glass pictures of Carolingian heroes and heard the Song of

Roland? Also, how often? One can scarcely even guess, but at least it offers the opportunity to create a picture of the net cumulative effect of exposure to multiple media in a medieval situation, and so appreciate the effect of propaganda exposure even in a period such as that which has been traditionally described as almost devoid of mass media. While rates of literacy are also impossible to estimate accurately in many historical periods, an overall view of media, and of the way in which a reading minority passes on the material it reads to the remainder, makes it possible to put this in perspective and realise that mass exposure to propaganda was not something which was born in the age of printing — let alone that of radio or television.

TYPOLOGY: OBJECTIVES

For the sake of convenience it is useful to divide propaganda into seven main categories, according to the objectives for which it is used.

1. Political: This covers all types of propaganda aimed at the acquiring or maintenance of political power. It includes not just the rival rhetoric of opposing parties, but the subtler forms of image projection which lie at the base of all political power. Tribal loyalty, patriotism, nationalism, civil obedience may all be means to this end. Flags and pyramids, triumphs and processions, eagles and anthems, crowns and tombs; all are examples of tools of political propaganda used over a period to foster dynastic security. Parvenu rulers from Caesar to Napoleon and Hitler have tended to be the outstanding practitioners but there are many other interesting examples from primitive monarchies and modern democracies.

2. Economic: This covers all forms of propaganda designed to persuade people to buy, sell or conserve goods, raw materials, fuels, land, money, shares. It includes the creation or maintenance of confidence, the economic equivalent of political image, which has proved to be the magic psychological placebo of capitalist economies. Its importance in relation to both deflation, inflation, the image of a currency, the image of money itself and the projection of acquisitive materialism or self-effacing poverty has yet to be fully appreciated.

3. War/Military: This is a specialist form of propaganda geared to demoralising enemies in wartime, encouraging the morale of your own people or troops, and winning allies. It includes leaflet bombing raids and surrender leaflets, prisoner atrocity stories, war cries and war paint, the dragon prows of Viking ships or the kill notches on a Spitfire. Strategic deception or the well publicised feint, the use of blitz-kreig films and Haw Haw's radio, or the Marseillaise and the Battle Hymn of the Republic, and hero cultivation from Pharaoh Rameses to Marshall Zhukov.

4. Diplomatic: This too, is a specialist form with limited objectives, usually used to provoke friendliness or hostility in a potential ally or a potential victim. Bismarck's use of the Ems Telegram to put the French in the wrong and his own people in the mood for war is a classic example; the Kaiser's telegram to Kruger is another; the propaganda campaigns of Hitler in the Argentine, of Lenin in Germany, of Britain in the USA both in 1914 and 1940 follow the same principle.

5. Didactic: This is part of social cybernetics, the education of populations to live together without friction, to combat disease, dirt, overpopulation, anti-social or unhealthy habits. Its increasing usage is part of the complex modern society, overcrowded and aware of environment. It has considerable power and in that even non-totalitarian states have adopted it, presents both a potential tool for further improvement of society and a possible tool for the reverse.

6. Ideological: This is at once one of the most exciting and dangerous forms of propaganda, concerned with the spread of complete idea systems, religious proselytisation. It often involves what Knox called "enthusiasm," the subjective, emotionally violent upsetting and rebuilding of peoples' minds. Prophets, mystics, Messianic flagellants, missionaries of all kinds are its practitioners.

7. Escapist: This could be classified as a form of political propaganda but has special attributes. Basically, it consists in the distractive use of media as entertainment in order to achieve social acquiescence; the bread and circuses of ancient Rome, all forms of spectacle, side show, organised voyeurism, cathartic mass relief or other communications which create passive acceptance or distract a population as opposed to actively

motivating it in a particular direction. It will often be found
being practised alongside censorship; indeed it is an indirect form
of censorship since it tends to crowd other forms of communication out of the main wavelengths.

MEDIA

It will be useful both to define what is included in the term
media and how media can be broken down into four main
types.

The first are the *direct* media, covering those situations
where messages are transmitted directly to an audience within
hearing or seeing distance of the point of origin. Within this
group, the two main sections are the oral and the graphic.
The oral covers all forms of direct speech message transmission
from originator to audience. In a primitive society this took the
form of ballad recitation, sagas, stories and simple play acting;
it was direct personal communication of material passed on and
adapted, but not necessarily written down; material which
fostered the growth of early monarchies, praised warlike, heroic
qualities and simple moral standards, and developed early
national loyalties. The graphic section covered a wide range of
non-mass produced graphic propaganda: totem poles, cave paintings, heroic statues and idols of Gods, all forms of religious
and political architecture. We shall see that these two early
media of propaganda, lacking largely the means both of
mechanical reproduction and geographical amplification, nevertheless were developed to an extent where bearing in mind the
lack of interference from other media they could dominate quite
large areas. In Egypt, for instance, there was massive scale use
of graphic media: pyramids, colossal statues, frescoes and
temples, processions, pageantry, all of which gave both its
monarchy and religion a highly potent and long-lasting image.
Similarly, as an example of deep and effective purely oral propaganda one could mention Judaism, which relied relatively little
on visual symbolism, but very much on oral tradition. We should
recognise that the graphic media still have an important propaganda role, though they can now be mechanically reproduced.
Stamps and coins sold the Russian and Roman empires; political
architecture still has its place; in 16th century England playing
cards carried propaganda pictures, and in revolutionary France

ladies' fans and men's tobacco jars did the same. On the other hand, direct oral transmission has largely been superseded by the recorded and electrically transmitted variety. Propaganda takes advantage of the economies of scale.

The second principal group of media (and it is really an artificial one created for the benefit of analysis) is the pyramid group. This reflects the need in primitive societies as they grew larger for some means of amplification of the oral or hand-written propaganda message, and the need for cybernetic organisation to balance the spread of military or religious conquest. Theoretically, this involves the Merton concept of two-step flow, where a message is passed on by one means to a minority and then by the same or different means to the majority. Significant rationalisation of this method of propaganda was achieved by the Romans with strict hierarchy and rotation of officials, responding to the difficulty of controlling an empire which was large even by the standards of modern mass media coverage. Similarly, we shall see how the Papacy utilised a communication network, and, more recently, the cellular propaganda technique mixed with minority media coverage has been successfully practised by both Lenin and Mao Tse Tung. This form of propaganda has the advantage that it is less impersonal than mere mechanical amplification and allows for two-way message flow up as well as down through the hierarchy.

Pyramid message flow is therefore a very significant part of the total propaganda story. In spite of the old standard experiments in message change, when messages were passed along a human chain to measure the degree of change, in pyramid situations accuracy was often maintained by very strict discipline such as that exercised by the Catholic church or the communist party during their expansionist periods. In addition the use of printed manuals, training and written instructions restricted deviation.

The third media category is printed paper. The invention of printing was of course an event of tremendous importance in the history of communications, contributing in a major way to the Reformation and later to the erosion of absolute monarchy. The Guttenberg Galaxy, as McLuhan called it, signified the reproduction and distribution of both written and illustrated propaganda on a large scale. There were, even before the development of faster steam-driven printing presses, occasional books and pamphlets, such as those of Luther and Tom Paine, which achieved, what today would be called, mass circulation. However, as will be seen, it is vital to beware of overestimating circulation and penetration in the early days, remembering that few newspapers could turn out more than two thousand copies an edition until the introduction of rotary printing in 1848, and that, for its first four hundred years, printing was a slow laborious process.

The fourth convenient grouping of media are the octopoid media of the twentieth century: those whereby the spoken word or pictures can be both reproduced and amplified electronically, thus reaching mass audiences very rapidly and with at least great physical authenticity. Again, the first impulse is to imagine that the obvious power of the new media: radio, television, cinema, must create a whole new era in propaganda. This is, to some extent, true. But there are grounds for not overestimating the difference which these media have made and for seeing the modern mass media not as a complete revolution, but rather a slightly speeded up version of traditional cybernetic techniques. There may even be some respects in which the new octopoid media are less effective than the more direct ones which they have partially superseded.

In reviewing relative media performance in historical situations it is also important to bear in mind certain straightforward physical, psychological and quantitative criteria. Physically a medium can offer all or some of the following: picture, colour, sound, movement, long/short message. On the psychological side, there are a medium's atmosphere and its authority or credibility. Taking the quantitative or statistical side, there are its penetration or coverage, its repetition rate and its selectivity. All these characteristics are evaluated in modern media studies and while in a historical situation our measurements may be cruder, at least some assessment is usually possible. In addition there may be some room for comment on duplication or overlap between different media.

MESSAGE — BY STYLE, STRUCTURE AND THEME

While content analysis from a practical point of view is still in its infancy, there are a variety of attributes in any message which can be classified, in particular, basic differences of style, structure or idiom and certain standard themes. From the point of view of propaganda the main variations of style relate to the persuasive technique involved. Broadly speaking we could say there are three: the purely rational, the quasi-rational/half emotional, and the entirely emotional. In the case of propaganda using purely rational material the style is factual, informative or logical, and the act of persuasion lies mainly in the selection of facts favourable to the argument and the leaving out or discounting of those which are not. If the presentation is logical and reasonable, then it can be effective, though as we see in many political situations it can be immediately and completely counteracted by an equally logical presentation of different facts about the same issue. From this comes the tendency, as shown by most research into electoral propaganda, for people who already hold fairly firm views to be influenced very little by rational propaganda.

The second style category, following the quasi-rational approach, uses allusions and associations to lend force and credibility to otherwise weak arguments. In an analysis of propaganda devices for the American Institute of Propaganda Analysis in 1937 Doob listed seven tricks: name calling, image transfer, the testimonial, the plain folks approach, card stacking or the piling up of apparently bad information, the band wagon or exploitation of herd instinct, and what he called the glittering generality. These are, indeed, the hallmarks of the cruder forms of propaganda, but the concept of image association has very much wider implications. The use of architecture, graphic identifiers, or music, the use of all forms of symbolism covers a very large area of 'soft sell' propaganda, areas which are not usually recognised as being propaganda at all.

The third style category is the purely emotional, the use of subjective ideas projected with enthusiasm, real or artificial. This includes the emotive oratory of the great religious preachers —perhaps Wesley is the best documented. The combination of threats of hellfire, promises of redemption or salvation, plus in some cases deliberate disturbance of the emotions by rhythmic drumming or softening up with music, fear or artificial excitement are also characteristics of emotive mob leadership, such as that of some religious sects, Hitler and the Maoist Red Guard. It has certain affiliations with some of the Pavlovian techniques of brain washing as shown by Sargant. In this type of propaganda the constant repetition of emotive slogans without reference to fact or logic, but accompanied by the right kind of emotional stimuli, tends to have a rapid and often deep conversion success potential.

Turning next to the categorisation of messages by structure there are three broad types which correspond roughly to the three categories of style discussed above. The structure found in most rational propaganda is what McLuhan called rather disgustedly, the linear or logical style. It followed the accepted patterns of discipline laid down by appropriate branches of academic orthodoxy: particularly history, economics, philosophy and theology. For instance, Karl Marx used history and economics to produce one of the most remarkable of all works of rational propaganda — The Communist Manifesto.

The second general structure type and the one which corresponds to the quasi-rational style is the parable structure. This includes the use of basically entertainment structures either to put over a point or to sugar the pill. In other words, the propagandist can use the vehicle of the novel, epic, theatre, or any other creative form to produce palateable and effective propaganda. Very often creators of such art forms do not see themselves as propagandists, and yet often, either consciously or unconsciously, end up projecting certain attitudes either of their own or those prevalent in the social group to which they belong.

The third structure group and the hardest to define is that associated with emotional propaganda. Perhaps the closest parallel is that of ritual. Emotional propaganda tends to find ways of purging the mind, reaching an emotional climax and then implanting its real message. Thus the structure requires to have ritual quality, concentrating on build-up, climax and solution.

Within this basic categorisation of messages there are a variety of sub-structure types or characteristic idioms. These are essentially linguistic techniques which smooth communications, make messages more exciting or evocative or simplify ideas and improve articulacy. They include such devices as rhyme, rhythm, and all types of figurative language or symbolic expression of ideas.

1. Rhyme helps to make simple phrases more memorable, more exciting and seem more important. It can be as crude yet effective as:

'The E.E.C. Is not for me'	'When Adam delved and Eve span Who was then the gentleman?'
'Deirie, Deirie, Halleluia'	'Liberté, egalité, fraternité'
'Dieu le vent'	'Coughs and sneezes Spread diseases'
'I like Ike'	

2. Rhythm helps memorability and is useful for repetitive build up. Whether it is a revolutionary anthem, a psalm or just

"Nixon out, Nixon out, Nixon out'

'Ho, Ho, Ho Chi Min'

'Workers of the world unite, you have nothing to lose but your chains'

3. Alliteration is also useful in the development of mnemonics. For example the superb slogan used by Julius Caesar in his triumphal procession at the end of the Civil War
'*V*eni, *v*idi, *v*ici' (I came, I saw, I conquered)
or the German piece of male chauvinism:
'*K*irche, *K*uche, *K*inde' (Church, kitchen and children)
or from the temperance movement:
'*L*ips that touch *l*iquor shal*l* never touch mine'
and from the 1921 British election:
'*H*omes fit for *h*eroes'
and
'*V*sya *v*last So*v*ietam' (all power to the Soviets)

4. Metaphor: of all figures of speech used as a form of sub-structure in propaganda metaphor is particularly popular.

One of the outstanding exponents of appropriate metaphor was Christ, a master of the use of simple but very effective images; for example his 'house built on sand', the 'new wine in old bottles' and 'the seed falling on stony ground', 'the shepherd and his sheep'. In papal history we find frequent use of 'the seamless robe' metaphor to describe the spiritual power of the papacy. There was Bunyan's extended metaphor — Pilgrim's Progress and Mohammed's narrow bridge over the abyss of Hell. In politics, there are numerous popular images, for instance 'the ship of state' with all its variations; 'the dropping of the pilot' for the dismissal of Bismarck, the concept of rulers as 'steersmen' and economic difficulties as 'hidden rocks', the flippant reference to British politicians 'rearranging the deck chairs on the Titanic'. Battle metaphors too are popular — 'the fight against evil', 'soldiers of Christ arise and put your armour on'. There are also geometric metaphors: oversimplification of ideas into recognisable visual shapes such as circles, (life cycle, migration of souls); balance (justice); triangles; waves (economics and history).

5. *Similes* are also popular and Christ again used them almost as often as metaphors; his 'as a camel through the eye of a needle' and 'lilies of the field' were particularly effective. Another great practitioner was Ghandi with his 'Banyan tree' and other similes; useful, like Christ's for communicating to a largely illiterate audience.

6. *Personification* is regularly used in propaganda; it simplifies, gives audiences something concrete to love or hate. Hence the tendency to produce statues and pictures of beings who represent some abstract concept or group of people. The American Statue of Liberty, Uncle Sam, the Devil as a personification of evil, John Bull or Britannia and Marianne, the female personifications of Britain and France. The church becomes *she*. The use of animals to personify causes is also common, allowing as it does for a variety of pictorial uses and further metaphors; lions, eagles and unicorns are specially popular. There is the bear of Russia, the serpent of Eden, the dove of peace.

7. *Puns* and the use of word play; Krokotill for Tilly, Burke's 'ability is the enemy of stability', or the famous Russian pun on the word 'Mir' which means both 'peace' and 'the world' allowing Lenin a pregnant double meaning when he said 'I want *mir*'. Recently there have been the motor car puns on Ford and Lincoln as American presidents.

8. *Clichés.* In an analysis of sub-structure the deliberate development of clichés or the tendency to select special vocabularies for communication in high noise levels is particularly important. Just as in air traffic control, where speed is essential, interference considerable and accuracy imperative, a collection of clichés develops like *roger, turn one eight zero*

and *out* or *over,* so in politics or religion a series of clichés or stereotyped phrases are used to put over standard ideas. Often this is following the line of least resistance in communication terms. Hitler was a great user of proven stereotypes such as 'Lebensraum', 'Herrenvolk', 'thousand year Reich' and 'November Criminals'. Communism has produced 'Imperialist lackeys' and other classic clichés.

9. *Paradox.* The shock effect of apparent contradiction or surprise can be used effectively in propaganda. For instance, the concept of Christ as a pauper king.

Finally in a categorisation of message types it is important to consider the typology of themes. This does not correspond to the threeway division of rational, quasi-rational and emotional; the various theme types are spread fairly evenly throughout the three, with perhaps a tendency for more frequent use in the quasi-rational simply because that is the type which makes greatest use of image association. For the sake of categorisation, comparison and cross reference it will be convenient to reduce a wide variety of theme material to nine common types which are frequently used in propaganda.

1. *The hero or martyr:* Hero worship and the cult of martyrs have always been useful topics for propaganda exploitation and a quick method of gaining audience co-operation. Imprisonment has helped give a martyrdom theme for Hitler, Gandhi, Banda and Kenyatta. Jan Masaryk, Che Guevara, Trotsky and Horst Wessel were exploited as political martyrs. Martyrdom has been a potent tool in religious proselytisation. Sometimes if heroic qualities are harder to find they can be created, as was probably the case with Chairman Mao's famous swim in the Yangtse.

2. *Conflict:* What the Greeks called 'agon', the idea of a struggle between two people, groups or causes has always fascinated audiences and can provide propaganda that is both exciting, satisfying and effective. The gambit of medieval kings and princes in offering single combat to settle wars is one example. The basic David and Goliath theme appears again and again in the history of image projection by leaders. Castro against Battista, Mohammed's Medina against Mecca, Hitler against the communists, Charlemagne against the Moors, Buddha against himself, Churchill against the Germans, Garibaldi and his thousand Redshirts against the Bourbons of Naples, Kennedy

against the Republicans, the struggle of good and evil in Zoroastrinanism and elsewhere.

3. Revelation or surprise: This is the concept of mystery followed by explanation, the 'whodunit' strain of communications which is one of the most popular escapist themes in modern entertainment and also has an important place in the history of image projection. The Resurrection, the raising of Lazarus, the mysteries of Eleusis, the Delphic Oracle and the Sibylline books, Moses in the bull rushes, the last days of Hitler.

4. The Scapegoat: The idea of blaming the ills of society on the element with the worst public image and exploiting that unpopularity to make a régime more popular, is a familiar one. The classic perpetrator was Hitler, who at various periods used Jew baiting as the spear point of his entire propaganda effort and used his antisemitic programme to create many of the most important elements in his image-projection. Similarly, Senator Jo Macarthy used Red-baiting to create a short-lived but powerful period of political dominance. The Inquisition's treatment of heretics, the general persecution of witches, and most other examples of excessive interference with minorities show the same basic use of the scapegoat as part of an image-projection campaign. Both French and Russians used their former aristocracies as scapegoats after their revolutions.

5. Millennialism and Prophesy: Human being are always fascinated by forecasts of the future, specially those which offer a golden age just round the corner or a day of doom. Cohn has shown how important the idea of the millennium has been in the popular thinking of the Middle Ages and how it was revived in Hitler's concept of the thousand year Reich. During the period of the Crusades in particular the idea of a Day of Judgement followed by a golden age provided a platform for a lot of highly emotional propaganda, often accompanied by flagellation, hysteria and anti-semitism. But the same idea runs through from Isaiah and Virgil's *Aeneid* to Robert Owen's New Lanark Socialism and the tracts of the Jehovah's Witnesses in the Twentieth Century.

6. Crime and Punishment: Appropriate awards for good or evil, revenge, human punishment and divine retribution, the use of threats and promises for social cybernetics. The standard morality story pattern is adapted in innumerable different ways to persuade populations to follow moral codes and obey human laws. Again, the theme of prosperous immorality followed by hybris and downfall is one that has a strong escapist appeal and is satisfying, just as is its converse, the tale of the humble failure who eventually makes good. In the case of pride and downfall, the more atrocious the punishment, the more exciting, memorable and cybernetically effective is the tale.

7. *Supernatural:* Magic, fear of the unknown, the use of ghosts or giants, sea monsters or evil spirits, every form of imaginary phenomenon has a natural place in the repertoire of emotive communications. The more credulous and unsophisticated the audience, the more appropriate such themes are likely to be. In a modern society science fiction or similar quasi-natural themes produce a similar effect. Each age has its cybernetic demonology from Napoleon in the cupboard, back to the Golden Bough of Nemi, Reds under the bed, or the Yellow Peril. In particular the power of healing and the power to conquer death have been exciting elements in cybernetic magic.

8. *Self-Sacrifice:* This is both a theme and an objective in social propaganda. A government may wish to persuade its men that it is good to die for the fatherland:

'dulce et decorum est pro patria mori . . .'

(it is sweet and honourable to die for the fatherland) The Spartans, Romans, Germans, Japanese and Vikings have been particularly adept at this, but the image of glorious death in battle has been fostered almost non-stop by poetry, paintings, statues, history, novels, music and Hollywood. Similarly, it is useful for societies to preach a general theme of self-sacrifice for the tribe, club, school or nation. The death of Nelson, the Viking warrior going to Valhalla, the Kamikazi's reward, or simply populations tolerating poverty because their nation was winning glory. 'Patriotism may,' as Dr Johnson put it, 'be the last refuge of a gentleman,' but it is one of the first and most common of cybernetic themes. The image of 'duty' has been assiduously cultivated according to the needs of each society.

9. *Parody:* Humour is one of the most potent themes of negative propaganda. It ranges from the political caricature in word or picture form, thus drawing attention to weakness, as the poking of fun at Marshall Tilly's passion for sweets during the Thirty Years War. It is easy to reduce the charisma of an opponent by mocking his bad points, accentuating his physical

peculiarities, mocking his favourite phrases, repeating his clichés to the point of absurdity.

The above is only a general categorisation of themes and far from complete, but it indicates the main potential recruiting grounds for propaganda material, sources for creating what Boorstin called pseudo-events; artificial legends as background to attitude manipulation. It also indicates those themes which are popular as well as effective. Propaganda must attract, captivate and motivate its audience, so that a good theme must have both entertainment and educational qualities. In these cases we can almost talk of certain message themes having greater conductivity than others, though too much entertainment and catharsis may mean less motivation for change. The clichés of folk mythology (Lippman pointed out that theme clichés or stereotypes followed the line of least resistance for communication of ideas) have varying power of conductivity — capacity for attracting an audience, interesting it and moving it to action, motivational change or attitudinal stabilisation.

This runs in parallel with the new developments in the semiological analysis of communications material worked on by Saussure and Oliver Burgelin and research on the uses and gratification of propaganda by Klapper and Schramm. Both these lines of inquiry tend to place propaganda in the broader perspective of total communications and attitudinal control.

INHIBITING FACTORS

In a preliminary review of the factors in a communication situation which might be particularly conducive to making it fail, we find three main areas: message, media and audience factors.

On the message side the most likely failure components will be propaganda messages that are unintelligible, boring, or incredible. Factual propaganda expressed in technical or semi-technical terms is highly likely to be ineffective. One research project showed that, after two years of patient mass media explanation, a large percentage of the German population still did not understand their parliamentary system. A test campaign explaining the function of the United Nations in Cincinnati only succeeded in lowering the level of ignorance from 30%

C

to 28%. Linguistic or semiological obscurity is therefore a primary inhibiting factor in any propaganda. As an example of lack of credibility there is the French war slogan of 1940. 'We shall win because we are stronger'.

The second enemy is boredom; propaganda which lacks any emotive ritual or entertainment theme tends only to appeal to the minority who appreciate logic or are otherwise motivated to meet the propagandist half way. Majorities, as Worthington put it, are controlled by manipulating their instincts and emotions rather than by changing their reasonings.

In addition to unintelligible and boring propaganda messages there are the problems of too much information, confusing messages, or rational messages which lack any motivational force. For example, logically argued campaigns against racial prejudice tried in both India and the USA have had poor results.

In Great Britain in 1940, Mass Observation reported forty-eight different posters, including the following fourteen messages:

> to eat National Wholemeal Bread
> not to waste food
> to keep your children in the country
> to know where your rest centre is
> how to behave in an air raid shelter
> to look out in the black-out
> to look out for poisonous gas
> to carry your gas mask always
> to join the AFS
> to fall in with the fire bomb fighters
> to register for Civil Defence duties
> to help build a plane
> to recruit for the ATC
> to save for victory

The cumulative effect seemed to increase resistance to propaganda and reduce its credibility.

On the audience side there are a number of significant inhibiting factors. As Miller put it 'Man is a miserable component in a communications system. He has a narrow bandwidth, is expensive to maintain and sleeps eight hours out of twenty four'. Not only are there limits on literacy, intelligence and memory but there are artificially imposed inhibitors such as scepticism induced by previous propaganda. In spite of Plato's recommendation in his *Republic* to use good lies for the masses, history shows that direct untruth usually makes poor propaganda, because once having exploited the credulity of an audience and been caught at it, a lying source of propaganda is rarely trusted again. This was shown in the latter days of Hitler when even the horoscopes in the newspapers had to be used to hide propaganda messages because the remainder of the paper was no longer trusted. It was also shown when Gaullist television lost credibility because of over-use for party propaganda.

The other factor in credulity is prejudice. Maguire has written about the effects of new messages on a prejudiced audience. Basically, it either ignores the messages or distorts their meaning so that they fit in with its preconceived ideas. This points to the extreme difficulty for any propagandist in putting over ideas which conflict with the beliefs and attitudes of his audience created by successive generations of previous propaganda (what is tradition but second hand propaganda?). It is because of the deeper long term effects of prolonged propaganda, compared with short term campaigns, that there is a tendency for attitudes to be self-perpetuating and audiences apparently conservative. It is perhaps because of this that when there is a very drastic change in propaganda message, as for instance there was in Israel during the life of Christ, in Germany in the thirties, Feudal Europe at the time of the Crusades, or England during the evangelical revival, we may expect the propaganda to be first of all ineffective and then produce a violent and sudden conversion accompanied by some of the more emotive circumstances of mental preparation. In other words, when there has to be a really drastic change in attitude then there will probably be a long build up, a highly emotive climax or even physical onslaught rather as described by Sargant in his examination of brainwashing and sect conversions. These may be followed by the blinding light which hit Paul on the road to Damascus, or the sort of minor saga of deprivation and surrender with which Koestler described his conversion to Marxism.

The fact that prior exposure to different propaganda is such an important inhibiting factor points also to the potential of the idea of using propaganda as a form of ideological innoculation, and of training populations to develop powers of resistance against future propaganda by exposing more thoroughly the way it works. It also points to the possible greater efficacy of propaganda which includes a mention of both sides of the argument or subject and disproves or discredits the opposing view as well as proving or supporting its own. McGuire has recorded some experiments in this field, as have Festinger and Carlsmith in the rather more difficult area of prejudice and cognitive dissonance. Abstract psychological theories in this region are not particularly convincing nor as yet very useful.

INTENSIFYING FACTORS

While there may be methods of intensifying media coverage and while some audiences may be particularly receptive, the main factors for propaganda intensification lie in the area of message composition. On the media side repetition is of course a well known factor for intensification; Goebbels put it 'if you tell the same lie often enough people will believe it'. Benjamin Franklin, impressed by the effects of repetition in his pro-American campaign in France in 1776 said, '. . . it is not only right to strike while the iron is hot, but it may be very practicable to heat it by continually striking'. Clearly repetition suffers eventually from the law of diminishing returns, or overkill, usually because of the development of a boredom factor or the stimulating of antagonistic attitudes due to some feature of the repetition, but there is no absolute rule about repetition limits since it must vary with the nature of the message, medium and audience. So far as unusually high levels of audience receptivity are concerned, clearly it makes a difference if an audience has a particularly high level of literacy or other form of reception skill or if it is suffering from what is sometimes loosely called a spiritual vacuum. An audience suffering from *ennui,* or where the existing attitudes are far advanced in their life-cycle and lacking innovation, is likely to be more attracted to new messages because of their novelty. In spite of the general attitudinal conservatism noted above, there is also a discernible hunger for ideological novelty during the declining phase of an idea life-cycle. As Hoffer put it 'a rising mass movement attracts and holds a following not because of its doctrines and promises but by the refuge it offers from the anxieties and meaninglessness of an individual existence'. An extreme but perhaps significant view.

The main observable factors for intensification in message structure are:

1. *The source effect* is the effect on message credibility of it appearing to emanate from a prestigious or authoritative source. Hovland and Weiss have recorded experiments on this, noting a marked differential between the effect of anonymous messages and those from respected sources, particularly in the short term. Similarly, Zimbardo did experiments on purely irrelevant prestige factors like the clothes of a speaker, which showed that such factors made significant differences. Then there was the delightful Sorokin experiment where Brahms' First Symphony was played twice identically to a large audience of students, who were fed with a so-called expert view that one playing was much better than the other. 55% accepted the expert view, only 16% rejected it and the remainder hesitated.

2. *Intimidation or agitation.* Fear, like hunger, exhaustion or other forms of deprivation of security, makes audiences readier to succumb, and a variety of experiments have been done on the effect of fear content in messages, particularly in health and safety propaganda campaigns. There do not appear to be any totally conclusive results, but it is evident that fear is an aid to short term conversion and motivation, but may not be so effective in causing long term changes of attitude.

3. *Enthusiasm,* the lift from rational to emotive persuasion by ritual and artificial excitement. Some experiments have been done on this, for instance that recorded by Hartmann in Pennsylvania in 1935 when a split-run electoral leaflet was produced to show the difference in persuasion powers of an emotional or hot-sell over a rational or hard-sell approach. We shall see many examples of the exploitation of audience response to emotional stimuli, from St. Paul to Wesley, from Peter the Hermit to Hitler.

4. *Induced response.* Audience participation in propaganda. Some act of contribution has been shown to make conversion to or memory and retention of messages more likely. Public confession has often been practised as a preparation of individuals for conversion; by the Russians, the Methodists, the Inquisition, the Chinese and others. Simple responses too contribute to reinforcement in learning, the saying of *Amen,* joining in the anthem, even nodding or applauding, answering questions. Wilfred Pickles' war time crowd questions like 'Are we afraid

of Hitler?' and, 'can we lick him?' Another form of participation is drill, part of an overall conditioning process for unquestioning obedience to authority, used from the Falange to Black Power. In addition such responses help the propagandist, particularly in face to face situations, to test his themes and styles, to be more sensitive to the moods of his audience. This response and feedback situation is clearly much less evident in octopoid media propaganda. As Smythe commented 'with a decrease in feedback goes a proportionate decrease in the humanity of communications'. Hence, perhaps the recent tendency of the new mass media, self-conscious about their remoteness from their audience to invent artificial feedback situations such as the phone-in programme or the massive mail bag encouraged by Russian newspapers as an outlet for frustrations in a totalitarian state. Other forms of induced response include the writing of essays or the acting of playlets by audiences, both techniques used for propaganda laboratory experiments. Compulsory response has also been shown as an intensifying factor, one American experiement even having gone as far as compelling their human guinea pigs to eat grass-hoppers in the cause of communicology. Hitler's compulsory salute was an act of enforced compliance that would help the remainder of his message to be accepted.

5. *Bandwagon effect.* Research data other than on electoral swings is limited, but again it is fairly self-evident that when a propaganda message is seen by the audience to be winning approval, the members of the audience are more inclined to believe it. So conversion accelerates. There is a tendency for a swing of opinion towards what appears to be a winning majority view or away from a losing minority, because of the herd instinct. It can therefore be a technique of propaganda to create the impression of a majority swing even when this is not true; the use of plebiscites by Napoleon and Hitler or of opinion polls by modern political parties are examples. However, there is also a reverse bandwagon effect with those portions of any audience who prefer membership of the minority to the majority group.

SIDE EFFECTS

Most propaganda campaigns inevitably have side effects,

some of which may be more important or more long-lasting than was intended. Work has been done on uses and gratification of propaganada by Schramm and others, looking at propaganda from the view of what audiences actually get out of it instead of what they are supposed to draw. Blumler and McQuail have applied this to the British political broadcasting scene, showing that audiences may, in fact, want to learn about political problems rather than simply be treated as Pavlovian election fodder. Other side effects or bi-products may be classified as follows:

Polarisation: to some extent this is almost a direct product and sometimes a main objective. Propaganda does tend to make people take sides. As Lasswell has indicated, it tends to firm up tribal groups, nations, classes, castes and sects, because it so often uses the creation of these loyalties to feed its own orthodoxy and further its own ends.

Trivialisation: Inevitably propaganda oversimplifies issues, simply because it must cater for the least intelligent part of its audience and aim for mass persuasion. Therefore it often leads to the trivialisation or reduction to myth and absurdity of real truths. Crossman pointed out the particularly trivialising effect of television — 'the more mass the medium the greater the likelihood of reducing issues to stereotypes, visual and oral formulas which follow the line of least resistance in audience penetration terms'.

Tension: What the Greeks called stasis, a permanent state of tension or conflict and competition between groups and nations is an inevitable result of setting up ideas against each other, nurturing loyalties and manipulating to action. The gladiatorial aspect of propaganda, the excitement of the struggle reflects in the struggle of supporters which can often ensue.

Depoliticisation: As Enzenburger has pointed out, propaganda tends to limit self-reliance rather than foster it: It submerges the individual and his initiative with master dogmas and group concepts. There is the possibility of audiences tending to become manipulated robots when octopoid media reduce feed back and participation instead of intelligently motivated individuals. Propaganda has a tendency to feed on its own power and in the words of Acton 'power corrupts and absolute power corrupts absolutely'. While moderate propaganda may be a justifiable tool of social cybernetics, intense propaganda can become a tool for self-corruption.

Escapism: Propaganda can often be escapist, as religion can be 'the opiate of the masses'. McQuail said that news has 'a narcoticising dysfunction', in that it provides a permanent melodrama, a cathartic extravaganza of other peoples' misfortunes, a substitute for actually doing anything. There are what Schramm calls the compensatory gratifications of escape or deferred social reward. In the same way, the fondness of the media for melodrama inevitably tends to perpetuate negative attitudes — even propaganda in favour of improving race relations tends to emphasise the existence of a racial problem.

Education: The amount of genuine education achieved in the course of propaganda ends may frequently be minimal, but it can often be considerable and should not be ignored. The Jesuits were propagandists first, but also very successful educationists. The Hitler Youth and the Komsomol are other examples.

Sleeper effects: It may not strictly be a bi-product, but it is worth mentioning the number of possibilities of post-communciation changes in opinion, where latent propaganda effects can be triggered off by subsequent events or influences.

Deviation: Not so much a bi-product as a miss-product. All propaganda confuses some of its audiences, partially persuades or incorrectly persuades and thus produces heresies, deviant ideologies. Marxism has deviated often in its course, producing many other heresies apart from Menshevism and Trotskyism. Sometimes they are genuine adaptions from the original, but often changes due to the complexity of the original message, as it is true of heresies like Arianism in the history of early Christianity.

CRITERIA OF PENETRATION

At the present moment it is difficult to outline any general principles for evaluating the penetration of propaganda.

There are certain forms of primitive qualitative and quantitive research which can be applied to current campaigns: recall techniques, both prompted and unprompted or attitude barometer surveys measuring results over a longer period before, during and after exposure to campaigns.

What is lacking is research into the permanence or impermanence of attitudinal change attributable to specific media or messages. Also lacking is research into the contribution of media to two-step conversion, i.e. the preparation of audiences by background propaganda when the actual attitude change results from personal follow-up at a later period.

Similarly more definitive research is needed on the precise effects of repetition including those of different spreads and frequencies of repetition; research into the significance of what is loosely called impact as opposed to the invisible wall-paper type of propaganda, a complete visual and oral environment of symbolism with innumerable subtle attitude hints buried in their fabric.

AUDIENCE ANALYSIS

In a historical study of propaganda it is important to be aware of variations in size, type and reaction characteristics of audiences. First, we can look at likely demographic variations. Propaganda can be deployed with specific target audiences or publics in mind or spread indiscriminately. It is important to bear in mind their make-up in terms of sex, class, age, literacy level or education. Beyond that, there are more specific psychological characteristics which particularly effect message penetration. Amongst these, which have yet to be thoroughly researched even in a modern propaganda context, are credulity or susceptibility levels, which can vary from one group to another. Then there are differences of perception or intelligence with possible subdivisions of this difference relating to the oral or visual media. There are also the artificial effects of previous or current message exposure from other sources. Lastly, and again as yet little researched, there are variations of persuasibility. There is the traditional strong resistance of the strong-minded extrovert to unwelcome propaganda, compared with the easy conquest of the more readily impressed introvert; but such comparisons are superficial, particularly in a crowd context. McGuire has done some work on testing persuasibility variables.

Cox and Bauer showed the greater susceptibility of low-confidence women compared with high-confidence women. Gollob and Dittes showed that conceit characteristics increased or decreased persuasibility depending on the type of message. Snedfield and Vernon showed that sensory deprivation had a variable effect on attitude manipulation according to mental type. Clearly, individual personality differences, the sum or average of these when they are present in a large spread out audience, and the same when put together in a crowd or mob situation, all offer different possibilities. While these are as yet relatively unexplored, in a modern context, some observations can be made in reviewing historical examples.

RESPONSE ANALYSIS

Active response can be a significant aid in producing propaganda results and a response of some kind is the normal objective of all propaganda. For the sake of convenience five stages of response can be isolated.

1. Attention, conscious or unconscious. Obviously initial attention to a message is the pre-requisite for further communication.

2. Attraction or interest in the message, taking the audience on from the first seconds of attention to pay heed to the remainder of the message. Achieving attention, may involve shouting metaphorically or waving a flag, whereas attraction involves offering something. Whereas attention may simply involve an involuntary shift by an audience from one subject to another or from nothing to something, attraction implies a more than momentary shift, and suggests that the audience has, after giving involuntary attention, now had the time to make a choice between staying with the new wavelength and going back to its previous subject. It also implies the beginnings of at least partial concentration on the new subject.

3. Understanding. The audience's attention has now been achieved and real communication can take place. While simple reminders or repeat messages can be put over in the first two stages, anything less superficial requires the third stage, although the understanding can, of course, be emotional as well as rational.

4. Participation, the first element of active response. Physically this can take the forms of answer or acknowledgement, nodding, saying amen, repeating the message after the communicator, reacting with tears or laughter, sympathising or identifying with characters in the message, or rationally working out the answer to the portions of the syllogism provided by the communicator. Research shows that this participation intensifies the penetration of the message and improves retention. The experiments involving essay writing mentioned above or other methods of regurgitation practised in education are examples. Communication which encourages participation is likely to be more successful than one-sided projection, just as question and response is practised effectively in teaching.

5. Post-message behaviour. This can take a variety of forms which should only be evaluated in terms of the post-message response at which the communicator was aiming. This could be a specific action or non-action, for example fighting for fatherland or giving up smoking. Or it might simply be an attitudinal change, a small step in altering the audiences' residual image of a specific idea or person. Or, the remembering of some verbal or graphic theme; or only the willingness to accept subsequent messages from the same communicator. Thus the required response, at this stage, can vary from some token of instant obedience to the tiniest element in a long process of mental or emotional conditioning.

In attempting to summarise the current stage of thinking on social cybernetics, we can see that the mass conditioning of human populations is a very long, immensely complex process, in which the power of individual communicators or media or types of message should not be overestimated. It is not easy to achieve even moderate attitudinal changes without years of multi-media indoctrination. Highly emotive conversion methods can achieve such changes in certain circumstances but these are rare and the results even then are often temporary. But while there is little need for panic about powers of the new media we might remember that the old ones were often just as powerful. It is evident that many aspects of media exploitation have not been properly researched and we need to know a lot more about the wider range of tools employed in the cultivation of public belief systems. Too often, studies have dwelt only on education, or mass media or the arts, and not tried to embrace all aspects of oral and visual expression which make up the total pattern of message flow to each audience.

Associated, to some extent, with the themes and images of persuasion are three particularly prevalent attitudes. These three have an apparent built-in attraction which makes them potential mass obsessions, and there are many examples of propaganda which exaggerate the attitude change it requires, in the belief that, taking a concept to extremes ensures good results. Emerson, on medieval propaganda, pointed out that the idea of chivalry was an extreme, but only an extreme idea would have penetrated in the Middle Ages. Besides, an attitude change which becomes a mass obsession has certain dynamic qualities which make it a driving force in society, the fanaticism of some making up for the half-heartedness of others. The typical obsessions of various eras have certain features in common; they tend to appeal above all to human self-esteem.

The first, under different guises, is tribal loyalty, which, frequently fostered in primitive societies, tends to operate on the basis that our tribe is superior to all others. Whether it is to clan, family or nation, this loyalty is encouraged to be obsessive so that rulers can exploit it for maximum sacrifice by their subjects. This group fanaticism, nationalism or patriotism has driven men to remarkable lengths in different periods; to conquer, rebel, feud, resist. The survival of the Jews, the Irish, Poles, Ukranians, Palestinians and Basques, shows the ability of this obsession, once established, to survive. The appeal of being God's chosen people or the master race, the elect, the few, motivates and satisfies man's underlying corporate sense of insecurity. It tends naturally to thrive on the hero-worship of the chosen one from the chosen few. It tends also, because it becomes obsessive, to be intolerant, to despise the untouchables who do not belong. This intolerance in turn sometimes leads to making scapegoats and racial tension, particularly when accentuated by differences of colour or religion.

Another obsession, which is frequently fostered by propaganda in the interests of leadership, is asceticism, the encouragement of individuals to reject self for the sake of some higher objective. This, initially, takes the form of simple self-denial, a cybernetic trick of huge value. But in order to project self-sacrifice, the propaganda has to be pitched very often above target and as a result we find the propagation of obsessive self-denial, fasting, celibacy, masochism and flagellation. The military ethic of the Spartan warrior, the Samurai, the Kamikazi makes almost a fêtish out of self-sacrifice. On the religious front, we find the self-denial ethic exaggerated to the point of absurdity in the lives of the early Christian hermits and Hindu monks, competing with each other in excesses of self-mortification. Saint Simeon Stylites on his column deliberately encouraging the maggots on his festering sores; Trappist monks with their vows of silence. Also we can find the self-denial ethic taken to extremes leading to Puritanism and Sabbatarianism. The idea of saving money as a Christian attitude was, as Tawney has shown, in his *Religion and the Rise of Capitalism,* the basic ethic for the development of the free enterprise investment economy; but at the same time ultimately accentuated class division. The self-denial ethic, so often successfully projected by groups and leaders has in many societies been a significant force for good, promoting restraint, peace, stability and care for others. Sometimes however, as with all communal attitudes which allow a sense of superiority, it has spawned intolerance and absurdity. Chivalry, for instance, was a noble cybernetic concept, applying the idea of self-restraint to a military society, but again pushing the basically simple feudal requirement of loyalty to the ultimate extremes caricatured in *Don Quixote.*

The third, potentially obsessional attitude, which has been encouraged and exploited by leaders, is that of acquisitiveness. Empire builders had to project a lust for conquest to the subjects whose help they needed. Nebuchadnezzar, Alexander the Great, Ghenghis Khan, Napoleon, Hitler, the Japanese warlords — all these and many more took Imperialism to extraordinary lengths, creating a vast paraphernalia of motivation and reward for their followers, but above all fanning the lust for acquisition. Similarly, modern capitalism, because of its technological efficiency, tends to outrun its natural appetite, has had to titillate that appetite and provoke material aquisitiveness to the point of absurdity, using advertising propaganda techniques to create demand for unneeded goods, premature replacements.

ACCESS TO MEDIA

Before concluding this preliminary examination of the input and output of media, the various means by which potential communicators obtain access to the media must be considered. There appear to be four main sources of potency which make this possible; the first is physical force, the power to dictate whose voice shall be heard or whose writings printed. Thus dictatorships or revolutions traditionally make media control one of their first objectives. Often in twentieth century coups d'état has seizure of the radio station been the political turning point for one side or the other. The ability to control media positively, by using them, or negatively, by the consorship of other peoples' contributions, by means of force, ownership or direct political control is one of the most frequently exercised.

The second form of control is by means of money. Either, by bribery of media owner, indirect financial control, or purchase of space and time in the media on an advertising rate basis, or by paid for sponsorship of 'bread and circuses.' Lord Liverpool said, a hundred and fifty years ago, 'that no newspaper which could be bought was worth buying'. Throughout the modern capitalist world, profit motivates the weaker media to a venal subjection to communicators who can buy space, but in addition, there are many major media which subsidise themselves in a legitimate controlled manner by selling a portion of their space for many forms of paid-for messages. In the United States, commercial television space can be purchased for religious and political propaganda. In Britain, television and radio time can only be bought for commercial advertising or government propaganda of, officially, a non-controversial character, although political parties and churches are allocated free propaganda space on a proportional basis. There are wide differences in the formal access pattern to mass media throughout the world.

Access to the media can be through the possession of creative ability or entertainment skill. A writer or artist with mass audience appeal is of value to media owners either in commercial terms, as an audience builder or in communication terms, as a message propagator. The criteria for such access may be far from objective; the taste or commercial judgement of media owners, the fickle statistics of public demand, or an apparently arbitrary choice based on non-relevant reasons or feelings. Access may be awarded to people of low creative ability who nevertheless have sufficient skill to cater for some specific audience requirement. On the principle that what audiences mostly demand is often of an escapist, less intellectually taxing and non-disturbing nature, communication craftsmen using traditional cliché approaches, capable of routinising news and drama, may be given better access than truly creative communicators. Similarly, in media which are under totalitarian as opposed to commercial control, there may be a tendency to go for the line of least resistance with material to please government, censor or committee rather than audience. Even the mechanics of media production favour cliché regurgitations and routinisation of message gathering, collection and presentation as Tunstall has stated. Hence, it is difficult to assess how hard it is for new original communicators to obtain access to major media, or whether a really great idea, even if uncloaked in conformist clichés will surmount all obstacles. The ideas of Christ, for instance, although given great conductivity by the use of imagery and parable, overcame a highly inadequate system of media.

A final factor in access to the media, is speed. When media are governed by free enterprise and the need to compete for a share of the mass audience, to be first with a story or an idea is as important as the quality of either. Because of the value of the scoop in terms of circulation or audience building, speed in news collection or story presentation becomes an end in itself, The famous breakthroughs of Reuters in terms of pigeon deliveries and later transatlantic cables are examples. Sometimes quite trivial news receives exaggerated coverage simply because one or two communicators got it first and exploited their victory, or sometimes, simply out of media habit, because it has the stamp of urgency.

Before continuing to a more specific examination of the history of media usage and communication systems, it is appropriate to conclude this introductory section by trying to identify possible criteria for assessing the relationship between media skills and historical events. On certain historical occasions there certainly appears to be at least some causal connection between the communication skill of individuals and their political success. Caesar, Napoleon and Hitler for instance all had outstanding ability in terms of projecting their own image and exploited available media to the full. Similarly, certain great empires or movements have coincided with or actually risen to prominence on the strength of an expansion of media usage. The Roman Empire made outstanding use of limited media; the monastic movement, the Papacy, the French middle class in 1789, were all examples of an upsurge in media skills, though which was cause and which was effect is harder to tell. Many of these examples will be looked at in greater depth later in this book.

On the negative side, we can also often observe signs of communication incapacity coinciding with political failure or incompetence. The classic example of bad monarchical public relations was Marie Antoinette's 'Let them eat cake,' apocryphal or not. At a similar level, Tsar Nicholas II spent his advertising budget on ikons, secret police, military parades and tiny intro-verted masterpieces by Fabergé, instead of trying to project the Tsarist image effectively. In both cases, perhaps the lack of communications panâche was symptomatic of a general lack of ideas and determination to repair an ailing government. It is perhaps typical of declining empires and ailing régimes that an apparent reduction in ability to use the media often reflects a reluctance to talk in real terms to a new rebel generation whose hostility it resents and whose aspirations it refuses to understand. The Stuarts, the later Popes, the last great European emperors all neglected cybernetic skill, doubtless because their immediate predecessors had come to take it for granted.

One tentative conclusion which seems to emerge from a quick review of the role of media in history, is that the mechanics matter much less than the message. Christ's superb flare for metaphor and mass empathy compensated for totally inadequate physical media. Great ideas like Monasticism, the Crusades, the French Revolution, Communism, were able to win through without the aid of sophisticated media and won massive popular loyalty. This theme, if valid, casts doubt on the modern idea that men's minds are now much more easily manipulated than they were in the days of primitive media. It may even be that man is now so over-exposed through such potent media, that it is harder for a good new idea or exciting message to mature and then to penetrate. The new media may tend to cultivate false skills of speed and novelty, or superficial slick-ness, which ultimately mitigate against developing a sympathetic

understanding of an audience or an imaginative grasp of its
visual and oral articulacy, both qualities which won results
for great communicators in the past. At least the idea is worth
testing and may act as a counterpoise to excessive adulation
of the new media. In attempting a general communications
audit of certain periods of history we can try to distinguish
between the contribution of the media to events and that of
events to the media. We can also test the thesis that planned
cybernetics or the political myth is, in fact, the only 'real
politik.'

At this stage it is important to include a brief historical
review of the development of the main types of medium which
man can and does exploit for cybernetic purposes.

MEDIA DEVELOPMENT

Pure visual media were available to man before history.
He had his cave-painting, totem pole, war-paint, shield decora-
tions and other means of asserting himself. Kings and witch
doctors projected their images with a wide range of symbols,
visual metaphors and graphic themes. These were eventually
formalised in the heraldries of different nations and churches,
and came to be used in architecture, on banners, uniforms,
and in the myriad different situations where a society's leaders
can make use of one or two dimensional objects to display and
promote. Such displays, particularly those with a strong warlike
theme, formed a large proportion of the man-made visual
background for the attitude formation of primitive peoples.
Another factor in the growth of the symbol arose from the
fact that while representative art was difficult or expensive to
reproduce even in small quantities, symbols lent themselves to
primitive forms of copying. The cross not only told a story, it
was particularly easy to reproduce in picture or sculpture form.
The fasces of Rome, later copied by France, Germany and
Fascist Italy, were also simple rods and could easily be copied.
The tradition of heraldic animals symbolising power; the eagle
of Germany, Austria and bear of Russia was also fairly straightforward, and became stylised in various ways for multi-media
projection. Initials had the same advantage. The Romans used
SPQR, the British in 1941 had their 'V' campaign, the Russians

D

and the Americans made considerable use of them. They too, became stylised, sometimes almost to the point where the original meaning or long version was completely forgotten. Symbols of many kinds become part of the visual folk memory and their use so widespread that even without the modern octopoid media, régimes can use them to considerable effect.

The caricature, too, can be a symbol. John Bull or Britannia, the representative Irish ape, the American cigar-smoking capitalist with a $ on his hat, so beloved by the Russians, the helmeted Nazi, the Sans Culotte, all became part of twentieth century folklore and propaganda, cliché short-cuts to obtain understanding, while oversimplifying issues. Earlier caricatures were often more complex; the three-headed monster represented the Papacy sprouting Jesuits. The tortuous minds of pro- and anti-reformation cartoonists could put over quite complex stories with a big range of symbols and a minimum of words.

The application of graphic techniques has made use of a wide range of ancillary media, some peculiar to particular periods or of greater importance in some than others. Coins, for example, were an important propaganda medium in Roman times; more recently postage stamps have been used to similar effect. Though, both are now less important compared with the electronic media. Playing cards were a propaganda medium in Tudor England, ladies' fans in revolutionary France. The sides of buses now project images as once did the shields and armour of knights. Buttons carried messages in Napoleonic France and twentieth century America. Pottery once said more than it does now; weapons themselves were decorated. Now key rings and pen tops carry simple messages. Most of these media are in their own right probably trivial: our information about them and their effects is almost non-existent. Yet in any period, it is the cumulative effect of exposure to large numbers of these individually trivial messages which can be seen to build up into a significant proportion of the attitude-forming environment. Clearly, this is likely to be a higher proportion when major media are undeveloped or with non-literate peoples. Similarly governments or organisations who appreciate the existence of these ancillary media take advantage of them to back up or reinforce the message which they are pushing through the major media. It is not insignificant that the cross came to dominate medieval life because it was displayed in almost every conceivable medium, and in the same way Hitler made sure that swastikas were seen very many times every day in many different places.

Architecture should be included within the umbrella of graphic communication media. Traditionally, it has been given little attention from the standpoint of its use as a medium of propaganda. It is, nevertheless, of great importance. Buildings are capable of communicating awe, size, assurance, power, or dynamism, and if in a central or imposing position, can do this to a fairly large audience over a long period. Inevitably, in political terms, it tends to be a medium for the establishment, not the revolution, although a rebel hideout or catacomb can become a symbol, by means of contrast. Traditionally, architecture has played an important role in dynastic projection. The houses, monuments, fortresses or tombs of rulers have been used to put over a long term house image: the pyramids projected the massive dominance and permanence of the Pharaohs. Arches of triumph projected the military success of Caesar, Titus, Napoleon — and typically Speer designed a massive one for Hitler. It is possible for regimes to produce structures which are useful and also communicate the régime's beneficence, skill and responsibility — the aqueducts of the Romans, the boulevards of Napoleon III, the universities and cathedrals of English kings, the traditional hospital of the up and coming American senator, the hydro-electric dams of Russia. In democratic situations, there is the tradition of parliamentary architecture; the mixture of power and compromise in Barry's Houses of Parliament, the Capitol in Washington and the many other parliamentary buildings copied from them, down to the municipal prodigality of the typical town hall of Victorian England. Finally in terms of religious propaganda the various forms of temple and church have contributed considerably to the total religious message; the awe, sacrifice, asceticism, richness, beauty and power of the faith projected.

Paintings and sculpture too have at various periods been significant bearers of propaganda messages.

Sculpture offers in cybernetic terms a special opportunity to idealise and literally increase the stature of heroes or rulers. The Romans mass-produced statues of their emperors, the British put stone Victorias in every Empire capital, Hitler put Horst Wessel in stone, and the Russians made a colossus of Stalin.

In addition, sculpture offers a means of personalising ideas or qualities so that they can be given some reality for the masses. Judaism was one of the first great revolts against the graven image, God in the shape of sun or beast. The Greeks indulged in superb imagery in their anthropomorphic sculpting of gods, the Hermes of Praxiteles and the Venus de Milo projecting a magnificent human message in the name of a religion. Sculpting of the crucifixion and the Virgin Mary has developed a love/ hate relationship which has often divided the Christian churches themselves. So much a part of religious communication does the graven image often become, to the chagrin of those who believe that oral and literary media should be enough. Even without gods and kings, sculpture still finds a rôle. Representational sculptures produce their anthropomorphic Liberty, their Victories, their defeated dragons, their android symbols of resistance or charity. Even abstract sculpture, produced under the patronage of authority, can symbolise modernity, power or simply excite.

Sculpture as a propaganda medium is relatively inarticulate and expensive to reproduce or distribute in quantity, but crosses hung round necks, bronze heads of Mr Gladstone, and even the sculpting of coins show that it does have some applications. The standard humanoid statue was a useful medium for monarchs from Caesar to Stalin. On Chartres Cathedral the many thousands of carved figures in strip and cartoon style, told the complete story of medieval thought.

Painting or illustration in its various forms, is now easy to reproduce in large quantities. The word poster is normally used to cover the propaganda use of illustrations displayed publicly. Although wood-cuts or later printing made possible the distribution of pictures in leaflet form, up to the Reformation poster propaganda was either of the simple graffiti type with hand-painted words, as found in Pompeii, or painted murals in temples of important buildings. With the advent of printing we find, in the Reformation period, both the wood-cut illustrations and the type-set poster. For several centuries the wood-cut or engraving played a major rôle in propaganda. The marvellous monsters of Dürer, the splendid cartoons of opposing sides in the Thirty Years War, full of cunning symbolism and deadly wit. The Papacy could be portrayed as a many headed hydra: the Reformation illustrators had fun. Alongside these must be remembered other propaganda uses of picture display — the superb communicating power of stained-glass in a medieval cathedral, ikons, dynastic portraits, hung like Queen Victoria or Hitler over every decision-making desk in an empire. New establishments, too, made use of the formal mural paintings— David and other artists, in the French revolutionary period, had a massive output of paintings, many with political motives. Soviet Russia has its iconographers of agricultural and industrial progress. Also there stand out, certain great paintings which communicated specially well a particular message: Goya's *Shooting of the Madrid Patriots,* Lady Butler's *Thin Red Line,* Delacroix's *Massacre on Chios.*

Non-representative graphic design too has had its major contribution, as we have seen, to the projection of régimes and causes, symbols can form the key or link between all visual media. The swastika stamped on everything. The cross, originally representative, but ultimately a simple, enormously effective corporate symbol. The Fasces, the Hammer and Sickle, the Crescent, the Tricolour, the Stars and Stripes, the American Republican party's elephant, the Japanese Imperial Sun — all such symbols offer great value in terms of identification, repetition, co-ordination, reminder, delineation of boundaries and sheer emphasis of size. A multiplicity of crusading crosses on shields, or a Red Square display of lines of tanks or rocket launchers all with the Red Army Star.

So far as illustrations in mass media are concerned, large scale reproduction of pictures is a fairly recent innovation. In the Middle Ages the nearest thing was the assembly line illumination of manuscripts by monks; there then came the era of the woodcut and engraving. Apart from the hand-painted lithographic plates of the Toulouse Lautrec era, colour printing on any scale had to wait for the development of photographic letterpress and lithographic plates in the early twentieth century. It is only since then, that illustrations can be reproduced in accurate colour and large quantities. Nevertheless in broad historical terms, while the half-tone illustration has created greater news realism, the bold etchings and symbols of earlier periods were in many ways highly effective in communication terms.

Finally in the graphic propaganda field should be included photography which as a medium of communication, rapidly merged into print and cinema. It was photographs such as Robert Capa's *Moment of Death* in the Spanish Civil War, which raised the medium to a new height of emotive communication. This was increasingly evident in the development of cinema, from Eisenstein to Grierson, Riefenstahl and Renoir.

The art of direct oral persuasion is a propaganda form which reached one of its greatest peaks in the ancient world, with such performers as Demosthenes, Cicero, both propagandists for failing forms of republican government against new dictatorships. In this Greco-Roman period, even the theory of rhetoric was very thoroughly analysed by Plato, Aristotle and Cicero. The power of emotive, as opposed to rational classical rhetoric, took over with Saint Paul and the great preachers from St. Bernard and Luther through to Wesley. Wesley could preach more than a dozen sermons a day, day after day, year after year, and was well aware of his capacity to sway an audience of sinners to repent, even to make them faint with the power of his emotion. In other cases, this power of tongues has been wielded less deliberately, by Millennialists, Pentecostalists and Holy Rollers with a common pattern of emotional disruption, fear inducement and last minute salvation. Into this tradition, must also fall the style of Hitler, based as it was, on the rhythmic ejaculation of chauvinistic clichés, tempered by a very subtle understanding of the baser motivations of his audiences.

The amplification of oral communication and its reproduction, all came as twentieth century innovations — radio, phonograph, tape recording and television. Of these, radio has perhaps come nearest to reproducing the emotive effect of rhetoric, and in general, one might argue that the new inventions have not created the massive extension in penetration of effective oral propaganda, which one might have expected. Disembodied, removed from its audience, deprived of much of its atmosphere, deprived of the mob effect, the human voice tends to be less exciting, and the arts of rhetoric and hot-gospelling have yet to adapt completely to the change. Both oral preaching and political argument tend to be more distant and less compulsive when sterilized by passing through the mass media.

Within the oral context the power of music as a tool of propaganda is hard to exaggerate. Music, carefully used, has huge emotive and unifying power. The music of monarchies has tended to impress by size and magnificence, a builder of pride and loyalty. The story of the Russian national anthem is typical. Till 1833 the Tsars used the tune of *God Save the Queen,* then from 1833 to 1917 the superb Tsarist anthem, changing in 1917 to the romantic revolutionary *Internationale* and then in 1941 to the more solid warlike and traditional anthem composed by General Alexandrov.

In Britain, *Lillibullero* was one of the most politically effective tunes ever composed. In 1688, its chorus, *Lillibullero Bannenalah* were Irish Catholic passwords put together by Lord Wharton to foster panic about a Catholic conspiracy. In his words, '. . . . it cost James II three kingdoms.' *God Save the Queen,* written in 1745, and launched at Drury Lane to combat Jacobitism, was thereafter used in nineteen other countries as a national anthem and, as a standby, even in the United States.

The Marseillaise, composed in 1793 by Rouget de Lisle and packed with fine revolutionary slogans is perhaps one of the most exciting pieces of musical propaganda of all time. *Deutchsland uber Alles,* written for Austria, by Haydn in 1797, an an anti-Jacobin tune, shifted to the new Germany. The anthem of Czechoslovakia, a cunning blend of a Czech with a Bohemian folk tune, was deliberately composed to assist in the development of a dual nationalism.

Beyond the formal world of anthems, music has provided many propaganda signatures. Particularly as a morale booster in war: from *Horst Wessel* and *Lili Marlene* to *Keep the Home Fires Burning* and *Tipperary.* The bugle, drums and pipes have been used to get more mileage out of armies. Music has helped shape images: Lully for Louis XIV, Bach for Brandenburg, Verdi for Italian Nationalism, Smetana for Czech, Chopin for Polish, Wagner for German, Elgar's *Pomp and Circumstance,* the marches of Sousa and Strauss, *Imperial Echoes.* The music, too, of rebellion has been particularly important; a catchy tune could transmit itself without the aid of normal media reproduction; *Lillibullero,* the great popular songs of the French Revolution, like *Ca ira, Yankee Doodle* and the *Red Flag.* The underground folk music of rebel groups has been an important unifying and morale boosting factor; the songs of the IRA, the *Red Flag* or Garibaldi's romantic anthem for Italian reunification. *Figaro* was to some extent an opera of protest and Auber's *La Muette* helped to start the Belgian Revolution of 1830.

Music can also be an oral corporate identity, a signature tune, a repetitive reminder which can have Pavlovian repercussions in certain situations like the instant reaction one has to a police siren. This, combined with the basis of folk music in its true sense, the musical saga, the ballads of the troubadors, the chauvinist warrior songs of each country and period, combine to make music an important message-carrying medium.

The extensions of direct media belong to the pyramid concept. In default of techniques of reproduction, societies communicated with their peoples through a chain of human oracy. The great disadvantage of direct media was the limits on size of audience. Even a tireless communicator like Wesley, preaching several times a day could not get round millions of people. Hence the development of cellular structure for transmission as used by Christ or Lenin or hierarchies as practised by the later church, by armies, civil services and so on. The prerequisite of efficient transmission of messages, by this method, is a clear simple message which will not easily be distorted, an element of discipline to keep the intermediaries from deviating, and a high level of motivation to enable the process to keep going. Thus the pyramid favoured strong messages. From the point of view of discipline the letters of both Paul and Lenin provide numerous examples, as does the propaganda field-force of Chairman Mao. Apart from simplicity of message and discipline within the hierarchy the third requirement is undoubtedly an energising drive from the top. As soon as the enthusiasm weakens or the structure begins to fossilise, the hierarchy begins to outweigh the message objective. In modern media terms, the whole concept can be linked to the two-step flow theory: the use of selective media to propagandise to an élite, and then send the élite out into the field to convert the majority, backing them up with media support. It accounts for the special care to educational systems given by Napoleon, Hitler and Lenin, to the Church by English kings, Russian Tsars and Napoleon. The Romans used their army as a medium of propaganda, converting barbarians into Romans, just as Mao used the Red Guard as an instrument of propaganda. The Law, too, has often been used as a propaganda medium, indeed, in the broader cybernetic sense, always is. In the Middle Ages the Monastic movement and the feudal nexus provided two types of propaganda pyramid that were particularly crucial in a period lacking many other media. In the modern world newer forms of pyramid media are the Trade Unions, which have particularly good internal communications, and bureaucracies of various kinds.

So far as the print medium is concerned, there is no need here to elaborate on its characteristics or to consider at length the history of its technology. What is essential to bear in mind, is that for more than the first three hundred years of its development printing was a very primitive industry; slow and expensive. It was not until the invention around 1811 of rotary printing using steam power, continuous paper making in 1817, linotype and photoengraving later in the 19th century, that printing became a mature medium capable of mass penetration. Some publications earlier than this period did achieve remarkable circulations — Columbus' pamphlet on America, Luther's tracts, Cobbet, Hannah More, Tom Paine, but the vast majority of papers were printed in very small quantities.

In terms of the application of literary media to cybernetic objectives it may be helpful to review, briefly, the input of the the various genres. We have to distinguish carefully between the work of writers who have been specifically employed by a government to write biased poetry or plays, that of writers who c o n s c i o u s l y include a party line in their ordinary work in order to get partial patronage or other reward from a government, and of writers who feel strongly about issues and include a propaganda element consciously or unconsciously simply because they share the prevailing cybernetic attitudes of their peers. In the field of poetry, Milton was, at times, specifically a propangadist. Virgil subtly buried an element of propaganda in his work, Kipling could not help being propagandist, but did not really think himself as such. Good propaganda poetry is rare; Solon and Tyrtaeus in Ancient Greece, Virgil and Horace in Rome, Milton and Kipling were all essentially establishment poets. On the rebel side Byron and the Romantics had their moments, D'Annunzio was one of the poetic creators of Italian Fascism. We must also remember the contribution of folk poetry mostly to militarism and primitive nationalism.

In theatre most attempts to produce propaganda may have been quite effective in their own time but have rarely been more than second rate in dramatic terms and have therefore not properly survived. In the broad sense of attitude manipulation, the tragedies of Sophocles or Shakespeare clearly have a message, but not one tied to any specific cause. By its very nature a play is most often an experience in its own right and therefore cathartic in the Aristotelian sense; it restores attitudinal equilibrium rather than motivating to action. Lear, Macbeth, Phédre, Oedipus, all the great tragedies concerned with the big man's downfall, contribute obliquely to the poor man's willingness to accept his lot. But there have been plenty of ordinary plays used for propaganda. Cromwell and Mao Tse Tung both believed in theatrical propaganda, as did Robespierre. The Moral Rearmament sect bases its main propaganda drive on theatre, rather in the tradition of the medieval mystery play. Outstanding in propaganda theatre is probably Brecht, one of the few dramatists of real stature who was also a major propagandist. Spectacle falls into the same category as theatre, ranging from Caesar's triumphs to Hitler at Nuremberg. Even Gladstone used church bells and gun salutes to help justify his foreign policy. Pomp, which helps create credibility, can also induce fear and obedience.

The novel has, perhaps, been more successful as a propaganda medium of rebellion than of establishments. It is, in historical terms, a relatively new propaganda medium. Perhaps the first great such novel was Bunyan's *Pilgrim's Progress*. Quite a number of the great nineteenth century novelists used it for anti-establishment propaganda; Dickens and Kingsley on the social side in Britain, Zola the same in France, Harriet Beecher-Stowe against slavery in the United States. In the twentieth century, Soviet Russia has been the home of great rebel novelists; Pasternak and Solzhenitsyn; in Britain, Huxley and Orwell. On the pro-establishment side tend to be the lesser breed of warlike nationalist novels, blessing the adventures of self-sacrifice, the spirit of those who risk all for country or empire; Kipling, G. A. Henty, P. C. Wren, Buchan. Children's novels and stories have become of immense importance with the development of junior literacy. From Hans Andersen to Angela Brazil, from Grimm to Enid Blyton bourgeois values are preserved. Children's writers in Nazi Germany, Soviet Russia or Maoist China produce cybernetic entertainment for the young.

We shall see a number of examples of history being used or misused for the purpose. History, particularly in the days before it became fairly scientific, was a subject that could easily be distorted, sometimes quite unconsciously, to put over a point of view. Usually it takes the form of the writer portraying all previous history as progress up to the present or decline down to it. Historical similes are also popular. Hitler becomes Frederick the Great, Mussolini is Caesar, Napoleon is Alexander. Grote rewrote Greek history in the light of Victorian politics, Mommsen rewrote Roman history in the light of the German nineteenth century. British history has received the Whig and Tory treatment, most Communist countries have rewritten their histories; history offers one of the largest funds of factual material for propaganda that there is; heroes, folk origin, primeval frontiers, empires to revive (the Third Reich), glories to recreate, martyrs, successes and failures, trouble-makers (the Jews), precedents and anniversaries to celebrate. Burckhard shows how in Renaissance Italy the revival of classical history promoted power-worship and reduced respect for Christian humility. Wells used his *World History* to promote internationalism.

Other subjects offer scope for the propagandist, if usually less exciting; genetics for the Nazis, evolution theory and economics for Communism. Philosophy has also produced propagandists of high calibre, some more practical than others. Marx himself, dabbled in history, economics and philosophy. Rousseau, Hobbes, Locke, Diderot and Tom Paine were propagandist philosophers. The justification of human liberties, governmental rights and obligations, the limits of absolutism, the control and application of power, all have interested the philosophers, and ultimately their material is utilised by propagandists, often out of context. This is the material of which tracts are made.

Finally, in this section, we come to a brief review of the new octopoid media; cinema, radio and television. Cinema is still a powerful medium, though in penetration terms as a medium long past its quantitative peak. At its height in the late forties, cinema attendance in the U.S.A. was ninety million and in the U.K. over thirty million per week; the peaks lasted longer in countries where television was introduced more slowly. The real importance of cinema as a distribution medium lasted about fifty years, although in so far as television derives from cinema much of the transmission skill is still active. As a transmission medium too, it is probably one of the most effective of all; combining sound, movement, colour, realism and fantasy, and projecting to an audience sitting together in semi-darkness. Grierson, the Scottish documentary pioneer, particularly saw the potential of film as a propaganda medium. 'Hollywood,' he wrote, 'was one of the greatest potential munitions factories on earth . . . . it could make people love each other or hate each other . . . . a key to the mass will.' He compares the somewhat crude *Beast of Berlin*, produced by the Americans in 1917, with the more mature, delicately cybernetic *London Can Take It* of 1941. His own films, including the famous *Night Mail,* were based on the principle that 'the ordinary affairs of people's lives are more dramatic and more vital than all the false excitement.' Film had this capacity for making poetic beauty out of ordinary people. Hollywood in the period when cinema was at its height pursued a fairly middle-of-the-road cybernetic line, promoting the All-American virtues: respect for law, nation and family in a vague kind of way. The great examples of propaganda film tend to come from Germany and Russia where the objectives were more clearly defined, and commercial considerations unimportant.

Radio, like cinema, was a medium which peaked early in its history, but though it yields precedence to television, is not ousted so drastically. The main influence of radio falls in a thirty-year period 1920 to 1950; its first main contribution in propaganda being the spreading of the news of Lenin's revolution, though that was through military networks, not proper broadcasting. Radio was a very significant medium in the Nazi period, contributing enormously to the spread of Fascism, but even then it was beginning to show signs of the drift towards triviality, which has now led it ultimately to the status of a second class medium, one that is used for audible wallpaper; music, panel games, lightweight news and the phone-in programmes. The radio propaganda war has been brilliantly analysed by Asa Briggs in his book, *History of Broadcasting in the UK*. In terms of major attitude changes it could have worked well in harness with the Press, but has now, essentially, been displaced by television. Amongst the great practitioners of radio propaganda must be Hitler, along with Roosevelt, Churchill and Jan Masaryk.

Television was early recognised as the most significant new medium since printing. Between the end of the Second World War and the 1970's it achieved a worldwide spread of distribution; technologically it became able to transmit world-wide, instantly and with considerable quality. Like cinema, it can capture crowd reaction, turn drama into melodrama, project personality, enthuse and motivate, terrify and involve. It is prone to certain forms of visual clichés; the political handshake, the standing ovation, the violence and spectacle. It finds ideas and images harder to project satisfactorily. As Wedgewood Benn noted it tends to 'sharpen conflicts artificially, to oversimplify and sensationalise.' The Pilkington Report called it at one point 'vapid, puerile, derivative and repetitious.'

In terms of propaganda, television has perhaps not yet truly been tested. Because it has to be a government-controlled medium there has been little television of rebellion; it tends more to be the 'bread and circuses,' escapist or complacency inducing; even when it tries to excite, it fails to be open-ended and therefore tends to be cathartic and self-sufficient, rather than provoking to action. Nevertheless its contribution to long-term attitude formation is already considerable. Of particular importance appears to be the tendency to encourage a culture monopoly in that TV throughout the free world is dominated by American produced material. The minority material, because it is less glossily produced, tends to be excluded from the peak audience periods. With its forces for conformity, inertia and complacent self-indulgence, television could be regarded as the most dangerous of all communications developments.

PART II

HISTORICAL CASE STUDIES

1. Reconstruction of Aztec temples in Mexico: a remarkable early example of cybernetic architecture

2. Monument to the Soviet Cosmonauts, Moscow

3. Russian Communist use of sculpture; stainless steel statue in Moscow

ARCHITECTURE   SCULPTURE

4. The column of Marcius Aurelius in Rome, with its strip-history propaganda message from top to bottom

5. The Chrysler building, New York: architecture as a success symbol

6. Moscow Exhibition of Achievements

7. Entrance to Exhibition of Achievements

ARCHITECTURE   SCULPTURE

8. One of Julius Caeser's coins: the first genuine mass medium for political propaganda in history

10. Playing cards, a popular propaganda medium in the sixteenth to eighteenth centuries

9. A tobacco jar used to help to promote the French Revolution

12. Jacobin medals showing French understanding of need to repeat visual symbols

11. Commemorative medal helping to boost the image of John Paul Jones

ANCILLARY MEDIA

13. The standards of Roman Imperial Legions in the first century A.D.

14. The cumulative effect of massed swastikas in 1934

15. US Democratic Party Rally

16. A ceremony of the new
Republican Religion of Reason
in the Notre Dame, Paris, 1793

17. British Imperial ritual:
Victoria proclaimed Empress
of India, 1867

18. Typical Nazi ritual, 1935

Preußische

Kriegslieder

in den

Feldzügen 1756. und 1757.

von

Einem Grenadier.

Mit neuen Melodien.

Berlin, 1778.

Siegeslied

nach der Schlacht bey Prag,
den 6ten May 1757.

Victoria! mit uns ist Gott,
    Der stolze Feind liegt da!
Er liegt, gerecht ist unser Gott,
Er liegt, Victoria!

Zwar unser Vater ist nicht mehr,
Jedoch er starb ein Held,
Und sieht nun unser Siegesheer,
Vom hohen Sternenzelt.

Er ging voran, der edle Greis!
Voll Gott und Vaterland.
Sein alter Kopf war kaum so weiß,
Als tapfer seine Hand.

C 3   Mit

Titel und eine Seite des Inhalts von Gleims Grenadierliedern. Genaue Wiedergabe des Drucks von 1778 nach dem Exemplar der Verlagshandlung.

19. Music for motivation: the song book of the Prussian Grenadiers in 1756

MUSIC

20. The hit song of 1792: *The Marseillaise*

ILLUSTRATION

21. An early stage in the creation of Napoleon's image; the dashing commander

22. Napoleon's image moves a stage further, towards apotheosis

23. Dürer's *Four Horsemen of the Apocalypse,* typical of the millennial promotions of the early fifteenth century

24. The Catholics use caricature in the battle against Luther

25. Hong Kong Family Planning poster copied from similar British theme

26. Indian projection of ideal family size

ILLUSTRATION   POSTERS

27. The Fall of the Bastille: the visual oversimplification of the French Revolution

Boston Massacre. From an Engraving by Paul Revere.

PRINT

28. The martyrdom of Boston turned into pictorial legend by Paul Revere

29. *Der Sturmer:* a typical front page in 1935: note long anti-semitic poem with reference to Dachau

Der Stürmer

Deutsches Wochenblatt zum Kampfe um die Wahrheit

HERAUSGEBER: JULIUS STREICHER

Nürnberg, im Oktober 1935   13. Jahr   1935

Emmi D. endlich befaßt sich mit der Judentaufe. Sie schreibt:

„Die Raffe kann nie durch das Taufwaffer weggewaschen werden. Wer Jud ist, bleibt Jud und wer Chrift ist, bleibt Chrift."

Daß unsere Mädels auch dichten können, beweisen die nachstehenden Verse:

„Den Juden mit den krummen Füßen
darf niemals man „Heil Hitler" grüßen."

„Der Jude sagt: Die Raffenschande ist keine Sünd,
weil man dafür drei Stufen im Himmel gewinnt."

„Wenn sich der Jud auch taufen läßt,
er bleibt in seinem Glauben fest."

„Der Jude ist dem Teufel gleich,
drum braucht ihn nicht das Dritte Reich."

„Der Jud mit seiner krummen Nas',
der paßt nicht in die deutsche Raß."

„Der Jude läßt sein Maul nicht ruhn,
drum muß man ihn nach Dachau tun."

„O Jud, bleib ferne diesem Ort,
denn Hitler-Geift regiert jetzt dort."

„Der Jude ist ein Raffenschänder,
drum wehren sich die andern Länder."

*

Aus der Fülle von originellen Einfällen könnten wir noch viele andere Beispiele auswählen. Aber schon die

30. A British war poster of 1944 modelled on the famous Kitchener 'YOUR Country needs YOU'

31. Nazi anti-semitic poster

POSTERS

32 & 33. The British Labour Party General Election Campaign of 1963

34. The Red Parade in Peking; Poster 1965

POSTERS

35. The peasants applaud Chairman Mao; Poster 1965

FILMS

36 & 37. Stills from Nazi
Propaganda film, *Swastika*

38 & 39. Stills from
Kinopravda news bulletin
on the death of Lenin

This is not a continuous history of propaganda, nor even a strictly evolutionary description of its development. Certain specific events or people are looked at in varying detail, in more or less chronological order, reviewing certain features of media and theme exploitation, noting innovations as they occur, noting certain similarities, but not attempting any rigid comparison nor making any moral judgements.

THE ROMAN EMPIRE

The Roman Empire saw greater advances in cybernetic skills within a hundred year period, from roughly 50 B.C. to 50 A.D., than in the thousand years before and the thousand years after. Admittedly, this period owed a lot to the development of communication skills by the city states of Greece and Rome from the fifth century onwards. They boasted some powerful individual propagandists like Demosthenes, Cicero, superlative writers and artists. But the image projection of Athens, Sparta and Republican Rome was on a much smaller and less planned scale than that of Imperial Rome under the Caesars. Pericles in Athens had devoted a considerable part of his revenue to the deliberate cultivation of Athens' artistic reputation and the promotion of his type of democracy. However, an abler propagandist would have covered up less contemptuously the élitism and exploitation that went with it. Sparta and early Rome had a lot in common; a very strong internal cybernetic image of selfless patriotism and asceticism, but their cybernetic techniques failed to adapt when they acquired increased power and wealth. The new communications network of Imperial Rome was a gathering together by Caesar and his successors of all the media tools developed to date in the ancient world, used to their full to control a huge empire and to achieve a penetration of particular images such as has rarely been beaten at any period. It is not insignificant that two of the greatest communicators of this

E

period, Julius Caesar and Jesus Christ, achieved in different ways a penetration of their own images which has survived two thousand years.

The particular development of cybernetics in this period was due to a variety of reasons; firstly the conquests of Rome had created a large geographical area with widely diverse populations and a need for strong government. Secondly, not only was the government centralised, but it had the power and money to spend vast sums on architecture, art and literature, together with the desire to project coordinated corporate symbolism and impose its image as a part of its overall political and military strategy. Already the city states had created through sculpture, painting, building, poetry, theatre and rhetoric a message projection of high sophistication. The skill of the Caesars was in expanding and mass-producing this means of communication so that it was projected successfully over a long period to a very large area. At the same time, the audience's receptiveness was heightened both by a political and spiritual vacuum and growing scepticism with existing forms of government and religion and by the exposure of these people to most of the classical art forms which were now being used for propaganda purposes.

To look at the Roman propaganda achievement in more detail it is important first of all to examine the skillful use of image projection techniques by Julius Caesar. This review, like Caesar's Gaul can be divided into three parts; his public relations during the rise to power, during the switch from quasi-Republican to overtly totalitarian power, and the period of consolidation.

Caesar's rise to power was not straightforward, and was significant for its reliance on propaganda techniques. The main ingredients were projecting a military success story and use of terror tactics at home to soften up the population. The military successes were of course genuine, even if they were deliberately created to foster Caesar's political career; what was so remarkable was the wide use of media to boast about them. Coins, for example, were issued to celebrate his early victories. Coins were to become one of the most significant advertising vehicles of the Roman Empire. As Grant put it they 'were the only social documents which the Romans could be sure that very many people could see'. Emperors took great pains with the quality of their portraiture on coins and with the messages put on them. Even Nero lavished great care on his coin image as war-lord, priest and divine protector of the Empire.

Caesar's second medium at this time was the written word. His war memoirs, published as a serial to create interest in his campaigns at home, brilliantly written with the aid of Gaius Oppius. According to Grant the early volumes were the most potent propaganda ever written; certainly their style and timing were brilliantly appropriate, coinciding as they did with a period when due to earlier scandals and failures Caesar's image had plummetted.

At the same time Caesar was using Clodius to create an atmosphere of terror in Rome itself, to make his ultimate political ambitions easier to achieve. As Sargant and others have shown, this technique used by both the Nazis and Communists creates a highly receptive atmosphere for the promise of salvation and security. Meanwhile Caesar proceeded on his long term image projection; increasing the pomp and ceremony surrounding public office, dropping hints about his own descent from the goddess Venus and above all always exciting. He was extremely lavish in offering and paying for bigger and more blood-thirsty shows than ever before. In fact, this and political bribery nearly ruined him. There were five day big game hunts in the amphitheatres and sword fights to the death by gladiators. To all this, must be added Caesar's personal presence and oratorical technique. He had taken special lessons in speech-making on a Greek island. But the cultivation of hysteria was a technique of the new mob orators. His passionate, high-pitched voice, his vigorous use of gestures, the emotion-charged way he addressed his soldiers, tearing open his tunic, shouting, his sense of occasion in, for instance, choosing the banks of the Rubicon to make a highly emotional speech, were all part of this art. Lastly, in this period we can note his arrangement for the daily proceedings in the Senate to be published, a subtle manoeuvre perhaps to let the people see just what their legislature was spending its time on.

Between the years 49 and 46 B.C. when Caesar consolidated his power the truly masterly touch of his public relations is evident. This was the period of his massive triumphal processions. four within a single month at one point, each celebrating a different victory in the Civil War, each with a different style of presentation. The mere organisation of these spectacles, with large numbers taking part and large numbers watching must have been considerable, as it was for Streicher managing the

logistics for the Nuremberg Rallies. The triumphs are described
in some detail by Suetonius; on one occasion Caesar had eighty
elephants in two columns dressed overall; for another, he had
huge decorated floats with scenes from his battles carried on
wagons. After the annexation of Egypt his prisoner guest,
Cleopatra, was used to dramatic effect, and unusual captives
provided part of the spectacle. Even in Rome, which had seen
a lot of spectacles, the cumulative effect of four such massive
ones in such short space of time must have been considerable,
accompanied as they were by considerable largesse. As a climax,
Caesar had crowned one of his floats with what must rank as
one of the most verbally clever political catch phrases in any
language; I came, I saw, I conquered, effective even in English,
but reduced to three alliterating and rhyming words in Latin,
'veni, vidi, vici".

This verbal skill, combined with the funds and organisational
ability to produce spectacles and his remarkable overall grasp
of the symbolism of empire-building Rome helped Caesar to
create an image larger and more stable than previous dictators
of Rome such as Pompey the Great. Indeed his followers had
even organised the chanting outside Pompey's house of 'By our
misery you are great.' Caesar brought together the eagles, fasces
and other traditional Roman power symbols and added his own
personal myth. At the same time, his sense of publicity detail
is shown by a variety of other measures; he began new schemes
for manipulating the elections of magistrates, he ordered the
publication of the correspondence of the Senate — a sort of
Hansard — and he organised the writing and publication of
a new civil code of law.

The third and final period of Caesar's public relations campaign came during the last four years of his life, the period when
he leaned towards overkill in image projection, and yet in
spite of its contribution to his own murder was in fact helping
prepare a longer term caesarism which ten years later was easy
for his nephew to revive. To some extent, his propaganda in
this final period was counterproductive with the more intelligent
part of his target audience. As Oscar Wilde put it 'When the
Gods wish to punish us they make us believe our own advertising'. Caesar certainly seems by this time to have become
isolated by his own propaganda and less sensitive to public
opinion. Like a twentieth-century African dictator who weighs
himself down with self-donated medals, so Caesar overloaded

himself with titles, many of them with deep significance in Roman eyes: first Imperator, a title originally awarded temporarily to victorious generals, but transferred by Caesar to a front for political power (our word emperor derives from this moment of changeover, just as the titles Kaiser and Tsar derive from the junction of Caesar's name with the imperial title). He also called himself Father of the Fatherland (Pater Patriae), Dictator, Censor, Chief Priest and, in most years, Consul. He adopted many of the outward signs of kingship, though not the title. He put his statue among those of the old kings, he had a golden throne, he wore a special white fillet and obtained an outstanding horse, to equal Alexander the Great and his Bucephalus. This may well have been part of the build-up to a final adoption of the title king. Certainly a senator was briefed to use a quotation from the ancient Sibylline prophesies 'only a king can conquer the Parthians'. This linking of Caesar with ancient legends or using astrological tricks was a particularly interesting aspect of the way Caesar summoned up the mythical past to legitimise the present, but it was also a symptom of his inevitable megalomania.

Meanwhile, there was considerable pamphlet activity. Especially interesting was the cover-up operation on the Cleopatra front, where Gaius Oppius was employed to produce a pamphlet proving that her son Caesarion had not been fathered by Caesar. Sallust was publishing history books denigrating the old senatorial ruling class, and there were at least two poets writing on Creasar's side — Bibaculus and Terentius Varro.

On the opposite side, clearly, it was difficult to match Caesar's spectacles, his bribery, indeed his total propaganda machine. But the senatorial party did make some effort. Caecina produced pamphlets, and there were a number of underground poets, attacking the Cleopatra set-up. Catullus, a lyric poet of real stature, plus a number of lesser known ones, produced a variety of lampoons caricaturing Caesar's bald head and alleging homosexuality while he was serving in the East, lampoons which usefully lent themselves to being chanted by groups of disaffected soldiers. We also hear of a number of hand-painted slogans on walls and posters making sarcastic comments on Caesar's policies.

One of the remarkable things about Caesar's image building campaign was the way it continued to function after he had been murdered by the Republican die-hards in 44 B.C. Mark

Antony had been a pupil with many of the same skills, particularly in mob oratory. The sheer spectacle of Caesar's funeral with its crowds of professional mourners and dramatic pyre, the divine shrine in purple and gold, the twenty foot high monument to the Father of the Fatherland, the well-publicised sighting of meteors, all these helped to add a quality of mysticism to his martyrdom, to confirm his larger than life image. It also shows how masterly had been Caesar's tying together of the attitude forming symbols and legends of the Roman Republic with his own image. He had made use of what he needed in the old Republic; the Roman army, Roman religion, exploiting every available art form and every communications medium and every popular superstition or fear to create a coordinated programme of attitude revolution. This was what gave his military dictatorship, which was really not so different from the several preceding it, the power to outlive his death. In his total grasp of available media; coins his only mass medium, spectacle, his favourite, literary media including poetry and history, architecture and sculpture, Caesar has perhaps only been equalled by Napoleon and Hitler. His grasp of meaningful symbols and the psychological needs of all but the old ruling class were quite remarkable. Above all, in common with other parvenu dictators he had the ability to create events as legend fodder. The Gallic War was not only a book he wrote but was a war he created for his own benefit as the basis for his image, which he exploited to the full.

Caesar's adopted heir and nephew, Octavian, later known as Augustus, and indeed even that choice of name was part of his propaganda campaign, displayed a maturity and subtlety of manipulating power, perhaps less original than Caesar's but in many ways as, if not more, effective. Coming as it did, immediately after Caesar's effort, it provides an example of a sustained campaign producing long term attitudinal change in the Roman Empire. We shall see how he finally created a climate of opinion that accepted monarchical rule and had a new pride in imperial objectives.

His early propaganda efforts were mainly opportunistic, in the power struggle after Caesar's murder, first with the murderers and later with his rival for the succession, Mark Antony. We see him using his coins to establish links with Caesar. There was full exploitation of the astrological susceptibilities of Rome, the idea of a new golden age and a saviour about to be borne, a theme also pushed in that remarkable poem by Virgil, the Fourth Eclogue. Ultimately, the propaganda potential of the astrologer became so great that in 33 B.C. they were expelled from Rome so that the government could exploit its monopoly in that field. For the time being, any reminder of the divine myth of Caesar and his ancestress Venus was useful to Octavian.

The other important aspect of Octavian's publicity was the campaign to destroy Mark Antony's image, exploiting the mistakes into which the latter's infatuation for Cleopatra forced him. There were rumours started about the capital being transferred to Egypt, torture tales: the poets wrote about the danger of exotic eastern women to pure Roman heroes, and swore that Troy should not be rebuilt. All Octavian's propaganda was for reviving the traditional Roman mythology, a new disguised dictatorship legitimised by a camouflage of traditional symbols. Like Caesar, Octavian used astrological themes, asserted divine descent, adopted the same emotive technique in speaking to his soldiers, tearing open his shirt. He also collected titles, but more judiciously than Caesar; he chose Chief Priest, Father of the Fatherland, son of the divine Julius Caesar, and cleverest of all, Augustus, a word of obscure meaning with a number of semi-religious overtones, an imperial, regal sort of epithet, yet it was not politically tarnished like the word king.

This new Augustus was now given a detailed programme of cosmetic myth making. His statue was put up in every city with subtle hints of divine origin and royal status. His coins associated him with a series of successful projects, above all he chose as his main selling point the establishment of peace in the Roman Empire. One of his master strokes was the closing of the Temple of Janus, an act symbolising the end of war. Peace was to remain an important part of his cybernetic platform. At the same time, he created virtually a new religion to act as a propaganda medium, particularly in the more distant provinces, where his audiences were both more credulous and more in need of a concrete focus for their loyalties. The new religion was emperor worship; temples were erected throughout the empire to Rome and Augustus. This provided a useful hierarchy for local image projection and a subject for an imperial architectural style which in turn contributed to the overall image. The new cult became an important factor in the spread and penetration of Caesarism.

Meanwhile the campaign to discredit Antony reached its

climax. Ronald Syme, a distinguished writer on this period, lays particular emphasis on the role of propaganda in enabling Augustus to force a war with Antony so that he no longer had to share the rule of the Empire with another. 'Created belief turned the scale of history', he says, showing how the whole build-up to the battle of Actium was contrived by Augustus using a consistent programme of denigration of Antony, the possibility of his transferring the capital of the Empire to Egypt and his being too much under the influence of Cleopatra.

Once his rival was gone Augustus was able to turn his propaganda skill to more long term attitudinal change, and it was in this sphere that he began to show an almost unique new flair. He began to harness the artistic skill of a highly creative group for the projection of the long term objectives of the Roman Empire and the consolidation of its entire ethos.

The peak of this effort was in the field of literature. One of his most able assistants, the wealthy Maecenas, referred to by some writers loosely as a minister of propaganda, collected a group of poets. These included a number who are amongst the great literary figures of Europe — Virgil, Horace, Tibullus and Propertius. All four received indirect government patronage and all four for instance were asked to produce a state-sponsored epic on the theme of an ideal Roman hero with a divine mission to found a Roman Empire. Three of them turned down this offer and Virgil accepted. He produced the Aeneid, which ranks as one of the world's great epics. It combines superb poetic imagery with stirring propaganda, and is one of the greatest literary propaganda pieces of all time. Aeneas, the defender of Troy, sent by Venus to found Rome, sacrifices all in the long struggle to fulfil his mission, a great story, beautifully told with the new imperial message put over with such superb imagery and proud eloquence that even the most cynical of the Roman upper class must have found it hard to resist.

'Parcere subjectis et debellare superbos'

(To spare the conquered and defeat the haughty)

Not only was Roman mythology given new life but also it was linked symbolically with the new dynasty. All Roman history was seen as a progression towards the present and the whole process sanctified by divine will.

Virgil was such a perfectionist that it was said that he wanted to burn the Aeneid, but was dissuaded. It is most unlikely that his self-doubts were anything to do with the propaganda content. Before we leave him, it is worth mentioning two other specific propaganda elements in his earlier writings: one, already referred to above, was the millennial theme, the concept of a new golden age, which he and other poets did a lot to cultivate and which has often been successful since. (Hitler, also, did it with his thousand year third Reich, third because it was a revival from two previous German Empires.) Virgil's other theme, mainly found in the Georgics, is that of the simple country life, good husbandry and conservation, a remarkable subject for poetic propaganda yet superbly carried off.

Horace provided the lyrical side of the campaign — his poems are shorter and less dramatic, but nevertheless often very powerful. A line such as:

'Dulce et decorum est pro patria mori'

(It is sweet and honourable to die for the fatherland)

can still be seen inscribed on 20th century war memorials, so perfectly does it crystallise the most extraordinary of all cybernetic demands made by absolute rulers. State propaganda often tends to centre round the fostering of the self-denial ethic and this is it at the ultimate.

The other poets under Maecenas' patronage also produced exciting stuff, but it is worth turning to another type of writer, the historian Livy. It is not clear whether he was officially patronised, but his history of Rome is by any standards one of the great artistic works of history in any age, superbly written and as accurate as his sources allowed, but contains an overall concept of progress and destiny leading up to the Augustan mission, which may have been historically biased, but gave real body to the objectives of the period.

For all the style and quality of this output we must remember its very small circulation, even though batch production of books by slaves was introduced. We must also bear in mind that literary propaganda was mainly designed for the ruling élite. For the remainder graphic media were more significant. Spectacle, the massive amphitheatre shows and military processions, the new imperial architecture and the use of sculpture to idealise the emperor, all combined to provide visual impact for Augustus' government. The Altar of Peace in Rome was a superb pictorial idealisation of the achievements of the Empire. The so-called Monumentum Ancyranum, was the standard monument throughout the Empire carrying inscribed upon it Augustus' personal record of events in his reign. 'I found a city of brick and left a city of marble'. Augustus' architectural policy was as deliberate as that of Napoleon.

Finally, in terms of media, there was a steady increase in the use of coins for propaganda messages, and his planned policy of improved communications — better roads and better postal service. Overall Augustus' propaganda achievement was almost as considerable as that of his uncle Caesar. Even in his final years, we see the effort turned towards preserving the succession for his heirs. Unfortunately, one after another they died, so that the work put into boosting their images was wasted, and Tiberius who in the end did succeed him, had a rather poor personal image. But in spite of a succession of unpleasant or weak emperors, the cybernetic skill of the first two Caesars had made sure that their method of government could survive the most appalling fiascoes. Even Nero, who early on made quite an effort with his propaganda, was not dethroned for a number of years. Augustus even attempted an anti-inflation campaign and one to encourage population growth. Particularly impressive was the power of this period to use great artists for propaganda without their being inhibited or producing mere versified flattery.

The final tribute to Caesarist propaganda is the repeated evocations of the Caesarist image which have occurred since, notably by Charlemagne, Napoleon and Mussolini but also to a lesser degree by almost every parvenu monarchy in European history.

Before leaving the Classical world, it may be worthwhile, as addendum, looking at the other extraordinary communications *tour de force* which came twenty years after Augustus at the other end of the Mediterranean — the rise and spread of Christianity.

Christ projected an image even more powerful in the long run than that of the Caesar family and the more remarkable in that his control over media was virtually non-existent. What Christ achieved to a remarkable degree was a brilliant linking of many of those themes and symbols which can be most potent with a human audience, so powerful that lack of media control was not more than a minor handicap. The fact that large scale projection of Christ's image was largely posthumous was part of his declared understanding and in itself, through the appeal of martyrdom, specially such a martyrdom, was one major method of overcoming the handicap.

It is worth looking at his technique in detail, and to call it technique need not be regarded as sacrilegious. The analysis of a piece of consummate communication skill is not incompatible with either accepting or rejecting the idea of divine assistance. Skill there certainly was and an outstandingly deep understanding of audience, theme and symbol.

The Christian message was aimed, to some extent, at a specific target audience: the defeated, the slaves, the less successful part of the population of the Roman Empire and its satellites. Christianity was positioned in the market, subconsciously perhaps, but it has to be remembered that there were a number of other competing and quite successful religious movements in the Greco-Roman world. As Barclay has pointed out there were around 60 million slaves and that in itself provided a sound basic audience.

Certainly the Judaistic system offered certain advantages to Christ. Amateur preaching at synagogues was normal, so they were an open promotional medium to any parallel new sect. The habit of open-air preaching with demonstrations, or visual gimmickry was accepted. Isaiah had worn a yoke, Ezekiel broke models, Ahja tore his robe into twelve pieces. In addition, this preaching was expected at times to be prophetic, in other words to come direct from God, and it was not unusual for it to have the rhythmic quality and assonance which could create crowd hysteria. Luke in the Acts of the Apostles tells of the mass conversion of 3000 in one meeting. Another aid in that direction was the habit of taking people out of the crowd and asking them to bear witness. This also Christ used. So, he was able to make use of a transmission tradition of sorts.

Next there was his capacity for structuring a message. Much of what he said was not particularly novel and the new bits were often the hardest to put over. But his total message structure system was unparalleled; his use of parables, his reference to Old Testament precedent, his sense of the dramatic — the scene in the Temple, the story of the prodigal son — his superb use of metaphor — the house on sand, the camel through the eye of the needle, the mote in the eye, the seeds on stony ground, the shepherd and the sheep — and a human metaphor — Peter, the Rock.

Thirdly there was Christ's understanding of the need for cellular proselytisation. The method of choosing the twelve disciples shows his belief in a totally dedicated group — like

Lenin later — who would carry on personal evangelisation in homes, through friends and contacts so that the movement could spread more and more rapidly, as its pyramid media structure grew. The loyalty of the cells was cemented by the rituals of baptism and communion.

Christ's sense of spectacle and liturgy was seen for instance in the preparations he made before his death — the washing of the feet and the last supper. Then his trial and savage martyrdom formed a calculated part of his campaign. He sensed that the ultimate projection of his message required some ultimate pinnacle of drama or horror, that suffering, martyrdom and a personal demonstration of his contempt for death would form the final metaphor of his doctrine of salvation.

It is worth noticing that up to this point when all the main mesage ingredients were there, Christianity still lacked any visual symbolism or any literary output. The cross as a symbol does not seem to have become significant until the fourth century by which time the Roman ruling class had become involved. Ultimately the cross was to become one of the most powerful and versatile of corporate identities, but in the beginning secret symbols used in the catacombs such as the fish and the XP symbol, were for secret use rather than display. Similarly, Paul's letters appearing some years after Christ's death were probably the first written documents, to be followed later by the gospels. It took several hundred years to provide the total panoply of music, spectacle, artistic representation and recognised text books which made up the medieval church. The early and remarkably rapid spread of Christianity without all that, shows the superlative message structure and audience sensitivity of Christ, and the value of the Roman imperial infra-structure for communications — with its common languages and interflow of messages, and the supreme adaptability of the Christian message. 'Blessed are the humble and meek for they shall inherit the earth.'

This dramatic reversal of status — the statement that the rich and powerful were less close to happiness and salvation than the poor, the oppressed and the unsuccessful had the communications impact of a startling paradox and the penetration power of a profound truth. Christianity offered a from rags to spiritual riches promise. It stated the problems with a vividness which few before or since have matched. It offered solutions with a compassion, an audience empathy which was quite outstanding; it had cybernetic confidence; the original charisma; a supreme example of spontaneous leadership rooted in a clear study of history.

In later stages Christianity often again provided the impetus for further outstanding efforts at propaganda. In some centuries it has adapted to new media better than others.

In cybernetic terms the ancient world as a whole can be seen as a period of remarkably large empires and widespread religions considering how primitive were its means of communication. Both religious and political leaders obtained a high degree of cybernetic control over surprisingly wide areas. Mass media with the exception of coinage were missing, but highly effective use was made of all the graphic media.

It was an outstanding period of propaganda architecture, sculpture, symbols of all kinds, processions and ritual. The image projection of the Great Kings, Xerxes, Cheops, Alexander, was splendid and awesome. In terms of themes it was a strange mixture; on the one hand monarchies and religions were often promoted by the exploitation of superstition, magic and mythologising. On the other there was a rational and often quite moving justification of self-denial, an ideal of service, which was promoted with remarkable sophistication by many states in the ancient world. In Sparta a uniquely strict military ethic was projected; in Athens a quite elaborate concept of communal service and reward; in Rome a highly disciplined concept of duty and service. From this stand point the achievement of Christ falls more into line with that of other figures in the ancient world who had successfully promoted the self-denial ethic.

THE PAPACY

This second period for examining a propaganda effort centres on the Medieval Papacy, particularly in the eleventh century. The Middle Ages are particularly interesting from the point of view of propaganda in that media were less well developed than the classical period. Transport and physical communications had declined in efficiency. There were greater language barriers. The struggle for survival against war and disease was so permanent. The literacy level was very low and media generally had regressed, so that a significant propaganda success seemed less likely.

The other remarkable feature of the Papal effort was that the position of the Popes in their drive for leadership of the western world was really so weak. Ullman has detailed the remarkable attention to detail with which Popes from Gregory I onwards, fought to project 'the hierocratic theme,' the right of the successors of St. Peter not only to rule the church but to take precedence over lay rulers.

For a long period the church, the Monastic movement in particular, had a virtual monopoly of reading, writing, public records, books and most forms of art. The main channel of message communication was the church, since its lay parallel, the hierarchy of the feudal vow was largely illiterate, less articulate and less regular in its internal communications network.

The basic media structure of the Middle Ages was hierarchical, pyramid; messages passed up or down the hierarchy and retaining considerable accuracy because of the vows of obedience or fealty they carried and the strict adherence to convention which medieval cybernetics produced. The messages were largely oral because literacy was low and graphic representation undeveloped or expensive to reproduce. We should mention that in certain graphic fields, there was considerable sophistication; the use of heraldic symbols to clarify political loyalties and Christian graphic styles to establish religious loyalties. Architecture reached superlative heights; splendid castles and cathedrals expressing the medieval ideals of leadership, both lay and clerical, showing it, at times, with awesome vigour, bearing in mind the lack of exposure of most of the population to other media influences.

Spectacle was naturally also an important medium in the medieval period. Ceremonies such as coronations and ecclesiastical investitures had enormous significance — details such as who placed the crown on whose head having immense meaning. The ceremonial of feudalism, the oaths of chivalry, fastings and penances, tournaments, pageants, exorcisms, mystery plays, public flagellations and the dance of death. These were the innumerable rituals of the Middle Ages; some on a large scale; some repeated on a small scale all over Europe. These rituals which took a symbolic form, were visual metaphors helping to form the communication network of the period. The characters too, were almost stylised symbols; the priest, the monk, the jester, the knight, each like the Canterbury pilgrims playing a ritualistic rôle.

On the oral front the preacher, priest or friar, was the greatest communicator of the period. But there was also the troubador or jester, travelling from country to country with the lays of chivalry. Between them, these two groups told and retold the cybernetic parables of the medieval ethos; a long repetitive, cumulative process of hierarchical indoctrination.

Turning to the specific theme, the projection of the Papacy in the period leading up to the Crusades, we can, first of all, review the cybernetic objectives of the Popes. These were to obtain and retain spiritual leadership of the Christian world plus a large measure of temporal leadership for the Bishops of Rome. We see from Gregory I (590 - 609) onwards in particular the development of a tightly controlled pyramid structure geared for leadership; he wrote text-books for his bishops, cultivating the monastic element and projecting the image of the Popes, as successors of St. Peter, the senior apostle. In one of the great papal metaphors the church was to be 'a seamless robe.' In addition Gregory made the conscious and enormously important decision that his church should take advantage of the revival of painting and exploit it for propaganda purposes. As so many members of the church were illiterate, he wrote 'paintings can do for the illiterate what writing does for those who can read.' For five hundred years the church was to be an immensely important sponsor for art, and art was to play a considerable rôle in firing the religious imagination. This can be compared with the Byzantine tradition which worried more about the idolatory effect of paintings and therefore restricted artistic output; Gregorian music was also extremely important.

The second Pope of significance in this field was Leo IX (1049 - 54) who developed the use of Synods or Lateran Councils to improve communications. He also used dramatic displays of holy relics to achieve extra effects on audiences, particularly when dealing with the vices of local clergy. He exploited the public confession idea in cases of simony by bishops. Both these methods of crowd manipulation fall into the enthusiastic or emotive class, but Leo was also a vigorous organiser, regular traveller and tightened the hierarchy by founding the College of Cardinals. All part of the steady development of what, Ullman calls, the hierocratic theme.

The third and one of the most exciting in our group of Popes who had an eye for propaganda was Hildebrand or Gregory VIII (1073 - 85) the man who actually originated the idea of the Crusade. He, like Leo, made use of both rational and emotional techniques.

On the one hand, the pamphlet war which he waged to retain clerical control of investiture was conducted at an academic, non-populist level, scoring abstruse logical points by reference to obscure precedents, some of them hardly authentic.

The projection of the hierocratic theme was to a very limited audience, to the ruling classes of western Europe, to achieve political ends. The opposition was equally recondite with pamphleteers such as Anonymous of York with his legalistic defence of the Divine Right of Kings. Only occasionally, did this advertising battle warrant wider coverage; Gregory's most brilliant piece of opportunistic public relations was the so called Humiliation of Canossa, where by various stratagems he ended up with his arch enemy the Holy Roman Emperor Henry IV on his knees on the snow outside Canossa, begging for papal forgiveness to avoid the disintegration of his empire. This was the sort of story that would spread with hardly any conventional media support. At the same time, politically it was perhaps too overwhelming, and counter attack had to follow. Gregory VII suffered for his success.

The other side of his papal projection was at a more basic level; encouraging mystical enthusiastic activity at the roots of the church. He greatly encouraged wandering hermits with their capacity for rousing crowd enthusiasm, helped by their wild ascetic appearance. He encouraged an almost mystic enthusiasm for improvement of priestly standards, attacking the lazy materialism of many of the clergy, just as Leo IX had done by a contrasting idealisation of young fanatics. There was some of this in the work of Bernard of Clairvaux and the Cistercian revival of the monastic ideal at this time. The crusading idea fell into the same mould, even though, at this stage, it came to nothing. Sometimes, this excitement of the population got out of hand, as, for instance, in Antwerp where Tandelm was so carried away that he himself claimed to be a new Messiah. It was one of the dangers of using crowd excitement techniques to stimulate religious enthusiasm that it could so easily turn into a violent anti-semitic or other deviant form.

So in the papal struggle for supremacy two techniques are used in parallel: at the upper level the Investiture Contest was a limited audience propaganda battle where the tiny number of copies possible of the pamphlets did not matter — very few could or would read them and only the attitude of scholars, senior clergy and great nobles mattered. On the other level there was the exploitation of primitive fanaticism which could be dangerous when it got out of hand. This came to its climax in the Crusades. Sargant, speaking from a psychiatric point of view, describes this period as 'the most violent and extensive religious excitement that history recalls.' Whether Urban II, the fourth of our propagandist Popes, appreciated that there were so many mystical undercurrents which could take up and twist this challenge we cannot tell. But certainly he quite consciously exploited them in the first instance. His launch of the crusading idea at Clermont must be regarded as the classic papal public relations manoeuvre, given that it was planned and Canossa was partly luck.

Firstly, in his launch of the Crusade, Urban had ex-communicated Philip, King of France, who like most rulers was being awkward over the investiture question. This was a dramatic move, good for setting the scene. Next Urban made his launch plans in France, not Italy, and in best hustings style announced beforehand that he was about to make an important speech with an exciting piece of news (Senator Macarthy was the other great exponent of this ruse). Next he set the scene. A large field in Clermont was chosen, a special platform built. Raymond of St. Giles helped with the organisation. His speech began with a long harrowing description of the atrocities committed by the Saracens against the Christians. He, then, produced a probably forged letter from the Emperor at Constantinople. When he announced the Crusade some key men, probably planted in the crowd, began to shout 'Deus vult,' ('God wills it'), a good chanting slogan. Next, the Bishop of Puy, perhaps also briefed beforehand, stepped forward as the first to volunteer and shouted 'I confess.' Cohn, who has made a special study of medieval political emotions, describes the tears and convulsive trembling of the crowd. More volunteers stepped forward and the concept of delivering the Holy City had been launched. Within weeks, according to Fulcher of Chartres, without any media, except wandering preachers, the idea of the movement

F

had spread throughout France gathering momentum as it went. Looking briefly at the message of the crusading idea we see all the ingredients of a propaganda success; the descriptive build-up on Saracen atrocities and the church in danger; the promise geared to a feudal audience of three years' truce at home if you went on a crusade, adventure and expiation of sins. There was the symbolism — the crusaders' cross, the battle cry/slogan 'Deus vult,' the vow ritual, the great battle hymns, and the link up with current mythological attitudes, in particular, the idea of the new millenium and of the Jews as unofficial scapegoats for any frustrations which arose. These last two elements were not intended by Urban II, but the inevitable result of his technique. As happens when subconscious emotions are deliberately excited on a large scale the campaign got out of hand. Peter the Hermit became an unofficial but very effective propagandist of the crusading idea. A wild ascetic riding a donkey, carrying a personal letter from God, frequently visited by visions, he was a very accomplished crowd preacher and could persuade audiences to leave home on the spot and follow him to the East. Similar, was Walter sans Devoir, using banners and psalms and the same emotive preaching technique. The cumulative effect of numbers of uncontrolled fanatics of this kind was a variety of deviant forms of the original idea and real physical disasters such as the People's Crusade and the Children's Crusade — mobs marching thousands of miles to fight, without any organisation or equipment. There were also the wild anti-semitic outbursts, flagellation and other oddities which persisted long after the Crusades.

The attitudes of the crusading period were also affected by the spread in the 12th century of the Chansons de Gest, the epic stories of Roland and Oliver as prototype crusaders of the age of Charlemagne, recited in verse by the trouvers or troubadors and spread along the Pilgrim routes of Europe. Huizinga, the great Dutch historian of ideas in the later Middle Ages, comments that the concept of chivalry which the religious wars fostered was 'a source of tragic political errors,' just as were nationalism and race in later years. He shows how the literary propaganda of the Burgundian court developed, putting a chivalrous gloss on ducal chauvinism. Dukes took on surnames such as Sans Peur or Hardi or Quiqu'en honque, similar to the deliberate romanticism of crusading policy. Offers of single combat from one head of state to another became 'peculiar forms of advertisement'. Usually they were bluff as with Henry IV and V. The challenge by the Duke of Burgundy to Humphrey Duke of Gloucester to prevent Christian bloodshed was a calculated boost to diplomatic and internal public relations. The careful preparations; pavilions, standards, banners, armorial tabards for heralds, the whole graphic pomp and circumstance of two conflicting identities, organised for the occasion by de la Borde show the subtle appreciation of spectacle in image projection by the Burgundian court.

The idea of chivalry, created with all its attendant mythology to legitimise war and to motivate for non-acquisitive war, was strong as Huizinga explains because it was so exaggerated and fantastic. Such bizarre ideas could get through any media. 'The soul of the Middle Ages could only be led by placing far too high the ideal towards which its aspirations should tend.' Emerson saw the same factor in cybernetics when he wrote, 'without this violence of devotion which men and women have, without a spice of bigot and fanatic, no excitement, no efficiency. We aim above the mark to hit the mark. Every art hath some falsehood of exaggeration in it . . .' Certainly in the Middle Ages exaggeration and oversimplification at times were needed to overcome the lack of media. It is particularly true of these two strands which came together at the time of the Crusades; the desires of the Popes to motivate a holy war so that they would keep the political initiative in Europe, and the spontaneous growth of chivalry from the previously inarticulate feudal ruling class, idealising their own way of life and legitimising their standards.

Before leaving the propaganda efforts of the Papacy it is worth mentioning the duel, that developed between Boniface and Philip IV. It was another pamphlet battle, with Pierre de Flotte writing on the papal side and the University of Paris helping out the king with new theories of theocratic kingship. Then for once the anti-papal side produced a winner in Frederick Barbarossa, of all medieval rulers the one with the greatest flair for image since Charlemagne. Frederick managed to turn against the Papacy some of the religious fanaticism and mysticism which had previously been their monopoly. Although papal propaganda featured him as the *'beast of the apocalypse'* and his Empire as Babylon, he won the support of many wandering preachers and himself purloined the Messiah image. He was the champion of the people against the materialistic all powerful church, an idea boosted by some obscure messianic deductions from Jeremiah which foretold the overthrow of the church in in 1260. When Frederick died there were hints of resurrection — a monk saw him go into the bowels of Etna — 'vivit et non vivit' — and the fantasy of Frederick's return was kept going for years. He became a mythical figure, the Emperor of the Black Forest, a potential saviour for the oppressed and a symbol for anti-clerical, puritan mysticism, a tribute to the remarkable image he had projected for himself while he was alive, the crusading knight in shining armour.

The other great example of image projection in the late medieval period was Joan of Arc who used the paradox of her sex and the mystical appeal of her 'voices' to capture the imagination of France.

To sum up the medieval period, it is only rarely in this semi-literate period that we see much in the way of planned propaganda. The papal effort in the 12th century was the most skilful and exciting. Elsewhere the image projection of most medieval rulers was limited to the crude display of force, decorated by identifying symbols. The apocalyptic deviants in the papal crusading campaign came nearest to showing the effects of emotive mass propaganda, but where the Middle Ages did excel was in the dedication of some of its pyramid communication structures and in the realisation of the power of art to propagandise to the illiterate. To appreciate the quality of medieval propaganda one need only step into a great gothic cathedral where one can still be overwhelmed by the image projecting power of huge fan vaults, infinitely worked ceilings, glorious stained glass, a total atmosphere which cannot fail to communicate dedication. Music was created to match.

Towards the end of the Middle Ages this led to what Huizinga called the extreme saturation of the religious atmosphere and the embodiment of this in images. Layer upon layer of symbolism and ritual were built up, masses in honour of the piety of Mary, of her seven sorrows, all her festivals, her two sisters, of Gabriel and all the saints. Hagiolatry drained off the overflow of religious effusion. Single images such as the cross and the lamb were no longer enough, and symbolism became more complex and obscure. Yet the Middle Ages retained that special understanding of art as propaganda. Theophilus, an 11th century Benedictine monk, wrote how an artistic vision of heaven would help with life. William Durandus was saying in the 13th century how people could learn from, not adore graven images which were necessary for an illiterate population. Even the Council of Trent endorsed the use of images as reminders. Above all the Middle Ages was the great period of the cybernetic dominance of visual art; painting, architecture, stained glass, calligraphy, heraldry and carving.

In reviewing the total cybernetic scene in the Middle Ages we see that what they lacked in media they made up for in intensity of message structure. This was above all the period when cybernetics was based on the projection of almost impossibly high ideals of sanctity and chivalry. Self-denial, gratification through service to knightly or monastic order, feudal lord or bishop, were given a mystical quality. All images were intense and obsessive, rarely completely rational; deviation, too, tended to be more extreme, intolerance more violent.

GERMANY 1500-1648: THE REFORMATION

The Reformation is remarkable in the history of propaganda for two reasons. It just so happened that these coincided; the first development of printing with moveable type on a commercial scale and the climax of a long period of restlessness within the Catholic church. In particular it produced one propagandist and media manipulator of outstanding skill in Luther. As Dickens describes it this was 'the first mass movement of religious change backed by a new technology'. The invention of printing was in Luther's words, 'God's extremest act of grace'.

Firstly, let us examine the contribution of printing to the Reformation. Undoubtedly, it gave a rebel group within the Catholic church, for the first time, an element of solidity and respectability. It also provided a sound basis, combining with religion to make good business and acting as a powerful medium. It was, thus, a two-way benefit; the Reformation provided the printing industry with its best sellers — at least half of all books published were religious at this time and the number of titles published in Germany rose from ninety in 1513 to nine hundred and forty four in 1523. The German printers therefore did well out of Luther and were able to invest in some technical improvement.

During the sixteenth century actual printing speeds were increased from around twenty sheets per hour to two hundred, still very slow, but with an average edition of a thousand copies, greater productivity was achieved. Between 1517 and 1520 Luther produced thirty major pamphlets, some in as many twenty-four editions, so that it has been estimated that over 300,000 of Luther's works were in circulation before the Diet of Worms. Only Columbus, whose four page description of his voyages had reached twelve editions had come anywhere near this success.

Luther's propaganda pamphlets were in the fairly new tradition of Fliegender Blatter or Flugschriften of about fourteen to forty pages with woodcut frontispieces, which had begun to be produced in large quantities at the beginning of the century. We know that Koberger, the Nuremberg printer who had twenty four presses, also had a sales force throughout Europe with catalogues of his publications. Luther's printers must have been similarly organised, as certainly Wittenburg itself with a population around 2000 would not account for many sales. His Sermon of Indulgence and Grace sold 14,000 copies in 1518 and 9000 more by 1520. His translation of the New Testament sold 6000 copies in its first year. The lack of effective censorship in the divided German states made this success easier, but it is significant that the Catholic printers did not do so well. One of their best pamphlets, Werner's *Great Lutheran Fool* was a little too academic for widespread commercial success.

Given the help of printing technology, the willingness of the industry to sell his works and the absence of suppression, Luther made brilliant use of his opportunities. His output was enormous, his style vigorous. He used plain German language laced with the common idioms of North Germany and Austria. He used woodcut cartoons by brilliant artists, such as Cranach, to caricature the Papacy and Catholicism generally. His mixture of Biblical quotations in the vernacular, folk wisdom and homespun metaphor gave his sermons and his writing the vigour for effective communication on a wide scale. There was also the relative novelty of his dialogue-type sermons which put both sides, and the dialogue pamphlet, which made for the more effective demolition of his adversaries. Wittenburg with its tiny population of around 2000 became not only the publishing centre of Europe but a training centre of great importance for the techniques of the pulpit. As Dickens put it, Luther 'had a charisma and a communicating power almost unique in modern western religion'.

Luther's message had meat to it as well as technique. Firstly the negative, aggresive side, his attacks on papal corruption, the buying and selling of church offices, the complacency of the monasteries, the humbug of clerical celibacy, all enshrined in his metaphor of the Babylonian captivity were bound to please most of his audiences. They had the classic debunking of pomp appeal. On the positive side, he offered a new native articulacy to the half literate urban populations, with budding consciousness of having minds of their own, a nationality of their own, a literary language of their own. Again to quote Dickens, 'for the first time in human history a great reading public judged the validity of revolutionary ideas through a mass medium which used vernacular language together with the arts of the journalist and the cartoonist'.

Outwith the use of sermon and pamphlet, Luther made use of other cybernetic ploys. His legendary nailing of the ninety five theses to the church door at Wittenburg shows the panache of a great public relations man. We also see the use of theatre performances to contrast papal depravity with the purity of the primitive church. There was his superb contribution to the propaganda use of hymn. There was the poetic version of the Lutheran doctrine put to verse by Hans Sachs. Further contributions came from David Jovis the glass painter and the whole school of brilliant artists led by Cranach, who were able to use both black and white, which could be printed, or colour which could not. Printed woodcuts, as well as pamphlets, enjoyed good sales — for instance caricatures of the Pope were selling particularly well in Nuremberg in 1523.

While Luther exemplifies the main characteristics of the new communications style of the Reformation, there are four more examples worthy of brief mention.

The first is not a Reformation figure, but a Holy Roman Emperor who showed more appreciation of the media than any other since Frederick Barbarossa. This was Maximilian, a Hapsburg who was sensitive about his image. In his struggles to get the backing of the German princes against both France and the Papacy, he gave patronage, at his court, to a whole group of artists and writers. Looking for an image blending latter-day medieval chivalry with Renaissance statesmanship, he commissioned the verse epic 'Teuerdank' and the prose 'White King', both idealised, thinly disguised biographies of himself. Dürer provided the visual idealisation and Sebastian Brant returned to the apocalyptic theme to give Maximilian semi-Messiah status. In all, Maximilian had remarkable success in creating a dashing, chivalrous image, although politically it did not lead to much concrete success.

There were a number of other Renaissance princes, often parvenus, who became obsessed with their own images. As Burckhard put it, ' . . . as they became familiar with antiquity they substituted for holiness and the Christian way of life, the cult of historical greatness'. A petty tyrant, like Astorre Baglione had Raphael paint him as a heavenly horseman and had the poet Matarazzo sing his glories. Ludovico Sforza had Bramante and Leonardo. This was a remarkable period in which the graphic arts and literature turned from God to the individual and also contributed to a fairly rapid switch in moral standards. Burckhard observed that, ' . . . political murder, vendetta and adultery became accepted components of art'.

Elsewhere in Europe the Reformation brought forth a number of new developments in propaganda. Knox in Scotland was a gifted preacher and writer with popular appeal. His 'Trumpet blast against the monstrous regiment of women' must rank as a substantial piece of aggressive pamphleteering. In England, there was also a new verbal ease. From Foxe's *Book of Martyrs* to Bunyan's *Pilgrim's Progress* there developed great tradition of religious propaganda writing.

On the side of the counter Reformation the greatest figure in propaganda terms must be Ignatius Loyola, who both intellectually and emotionally had a very shrewd understanding of human cybernetics. On the emotive side, his own direct conversions were associated with a mystic, highly charged fanaticism. He encouraged fasting amongst his followers, and met in a darkened chapel. Both techniques were according to Sargant geared to 'wiping clean the cortical slate and preparing people to reverse their previous behaviour patterns'. He followed up with a closely integrated cellular system, insistence on absolute obedience, and the superbly administered Jesuit educational machine, which became the prime propaganda organisation for Catholicism for some years to come. It was remarkably successful in restoring Austria completely to the Catholics and then achieved the quite amazing conversion of the Polish peasantry to Catholicism from Orthodoxy in face of strong Lutheran and Calvinist competition. Thereafter, they achieved notable propaganda successes in South America and China, where greater success was inhibited by the instructions of the Papacy not to adapt Christian propaganda for a Chinese audience. The Jesuits still provide a valid educational system, though their propaganda technique suffers to some extent from the strait-jacket of its original fanaticism. 'If the Church preaches that a thing which appears to us as white is black, we must proclaim it black immediately'. Finally the Jesuits were of course élitist in their choice of a target audience. It was through the conversion of pivotal groups that they saw themselves contributing most to the welfare of the church.

Two final examples of propaganda in the Reformation period both spring from the violence and political upheaval which followed it; the civil wars in Britain and Germany. First the British; Oliver Cromwell is, not surprisingly, the British ruler who paid most attention to propaganda in any period up to the twentieth century. Not only as a parvenu monarch but also as one, who was attacked both by the Royalists and the extreme Puritans and Levellers; he seems to have been just embarking on a major image building campaign for his dynasty when he died. The 'warts and all' attitude is a little confusing from the man who was preparing a new issue of coins showing him wearing the imperial laurel and with a crown on the reverse side. A 1659 broadsheet showed him wearing the crown. He had a fake genealogy drawn up and his title changed to Lord Protector.

All this shows a remarkable change from the semi-rustic, semi-soldierly image originally cultivated by Cromwell and demonstrates the sense of insecurity in his régime. This was in spite of some earlier propaganda works which in terms of literary quality must rank amongst the best in the English language. Milton's *Eikonoklastes* was an attack on hereditary monarchy and justification of regicide, a masterly defence of the new Commonwealth. He received a salary from the Protector and produced a number of other works to project its image. In 1651 his *First Defence of the People of England* put over the idea of the Commonwealth and his *Second Defence* in 1654 portrayed Cromwell as a kind of Old Testament hero who had provided England with well regulated liberty. In addition to Milton, Andrew Marvel was another poet of stature who wrote on behalf of the régime, perhaps more fulsome than Milton, and more attuned to the change in Cromwell's projection from a republican hero to a quasi-regal figure in the later 1650's His *First Anniversary of the Government under His Highness the Lord Protector* falls into that category. In addition Davenet was writing pro-Cromwell operas for the London stage, and the writers of the pro-government *Mercurius Politicus* weekly.

Royalist counter-propaganda was also quite astute. It was one of the few occasions when the followers of the Stuarts paid some attention to image projection. Another was in the early days of Bonnie Prince Charlie, for whom a most romantic image was created, though rather inadequately transmitted to most parts of Britain. The Royalists in the 1650's were making fun of Cromwell quite successfully; calling him Ruby Nose, Copper Nose and Nose Almighty. In fact satire was their most effective medium. They had two successful papers, the *Mercurius Aulius* and the *Mercurius Pragmaticus,* of limited circulation but prising away at the ruling class and undermining Cromwell's image just as much as the Levellers at the opposite political extreme with their pamphlets such as *England's New Chains Discovered.* The cybernetic effort of Cromwell cannot therefore be regarded as having been successful, in spite of the talented writers on his side. He was squeezed between two opponents and pleased neither side with either of his two images. Significantly, the navy's flagship the *Naseby* was renamed *Charles II* in 1660 and we are back with traditional British royal cybernetics: flags, uniforms, orb and sceptre. Some pomp and circumstance were all a British monarch needed, unless he or she flouted parliament.

The German civil war, known as the Thirty Years War, partly because the sides were ill-defined and because other continental countries backed one or other of the parties, was a war in which propaganda played a particularly large part. This has been well-documented by Belder, who describes the wide proliferation of pamphlets sold in large quantities in shops. A new development was posters printed from copper plates, which made possible larger numbers than could be achieved with woodcuts. The posters were sold complete with a poem at the foot and sometimes even music. Belder claimed, therefore, 'in spite of a low rate of literacy all classes of the population were reached by propaganda in the Thirty Years War'.

On the Protestant side, the French subsidised a propaganda effort, hiring a Father Joseph and Johann Stella to write on their behalf. The Swedes stole an Austrian gimmick, using the *Sued* spelt backwards is *Deus* or God as part of the image build-up for their King Gustavus Adolphus when he entered the war as a Protestant champion. Both the Old Testament and Greek mythology were raided for comparisions with the modern heroes of the war. One new epic poem disguised the current war as the Trojan War with Tilly as Hector and Gustavus as Achilles, the Protestants as the Greeks and the Catholics as the Trojans. The Catholic Hapsburgs were portrayed as over-ambitious, longing for world dominion. As the worst insults, available at the time, the epithets, Jews, Jesuits and Mamelukes were applied to them. Tilly, their main general, was nicknamed Crokotill, and his fondness for sweets was satirised in word and picture.

Both sides indulged in atrocity stories about the other. Of all the people on the Protestant side, who could be picked on, the one who offered most scope for jokes and caricature was Frederick, the ex-King of Bohemia. He was portrayed as the Winter King, the King who had lost his throne and had nowhere to go. On the whole, the propaganda did not reach a high level. Each side promised the towns trade, the soldiers booty and the population peace, warning of high prices and starvation if the other side won. So the pamphlet writing and illustration skill inspired by the Reformation was now used to make petty points in a long and disastrous period of war.

Perhaps the most exciting thing about the sixteenth and seventeenth centuries propaganda was the uninhibited cut and thrust between the two major factions of the period — Catholic and Protestant. Each side had equal access to media until one became strong enough to impose censorship. Because Catholicism was resilient, and rose to the challenge of new cybernetic requirements, the ideological battle was far from one-sided. The other vitally important feature of Protestant propaganda was its contribution to training for the political protests of two centuries later.

THE REVOLUTIONARY PERIOD

In propaganda terms the Revolutionary period in the last quarter of the eighteenth century showed a full exploitation of the techniques developed in the Reformation without any real significant changes. Literacy had increased marginally, the audiences tended to be larger, printing was technically a little more advanced and transport was more efficient. Towards the end of the century, steam power was available for printing; paper making machinery was developed, and cheaper print production made possible even wider distribution. However, except for best-selling pamphlets like Tom Paine or Richard Price, no publications really approached the penetration level of mass media (the UNESCO criterion is one paper per ten people). The real climax of propaganda technique in the period before the modern mass media was the French Revolution, but before looking at that it is worth comparing the use of propaganda in the English speaking world on both sides of the Atlantic in the last part of the eighteenth century.

There was an interesting development of political verbal fluency in the pro and anti-Walpole campaigns — particularly the *Craftsman* in 1720's and 30's. Also Hogarth produced his prints on the South Sea Bubble and the social problems of London, although later according to Wilkes, prostituted his talents to defend Bute. This was the period of development of Britannia and John Bull as symbols of steadily increasing cybernetic activity.

The controversy over the so called Jew Bill of 1753 in England provides a useful starting point, especially since the propaganda on both sides has been carefully researched by T. W. Perry. This particular Bill shows the two political parties of the time, the Whigs and Tories each mobilising the support of the literate classes through the traditional channels of Coffee House readership and pamphlets. In addition, because feelings, as ever, run deep when race is involved, it shows how, even in this period emotive themes could be exploited effectively and use made of other techniques. As many as sixty pamphlets against the Bill were published in one year, many of them quite long and some of them utilising crude and emotive language. The *Modest Apology for the Citizen Merchants of London*, which went to three editions contained, 'You know a Jew at first sight, his dirty skin, the malignant blackness of his eyes which bespeaks guilt and murder'. The *Oxfordshire Journal* kept up an attack every week for six months mostly in the form of letters to the editor, referring to the Oxford Whigs as favourers of infidelity and circumcision, mentioning the killing of a baby in circumcision by a Northumbrian curate. There were also a wide range of anti-semitic articles of varying subtlety in the *London Evening Post,* the *Northampton Mercury* and *London Magazine.* One of the papers listed all the art treasures which were supposedly in Jewish hands. It is significant when one realises that the real issue was whether the London City merchants who supported the Tories should be allowed to keep their monopoly or share it with the Jewish traders. Whig supporters who were beginning to have some commercial success. It was a commercial battle, and yet the range of racial hatred and exploitation of the worst form of racial feelings is reminiscent of Germany in the 1930's. In fact the propaganda technique was very similar.

At the same time satirical prints were being sold 6d (2½p) for black and white, 1/- (5p) for coloured; twenty five were available opposing the Bill, mostly on the theme of the Whig members being bribed with Jewish money to vote for it. The Tories also used their traditional private medium, the parish clergy of the Church of England, who were mobilised to preach against the Bill. They also began to organise the type of fringe public relations activities which have since become standard; political dinners, rallies with banners saying NO JEWS. The women went round wearing ribbons or crosses with effigies of Jews. It thus became a stigma not to wear some anti-Bill identification. The classic build-up for a racial problem.

The Whig counter-attack was more limited. They employed Philip Carteret Webb and the Reverend Josiah Tucker to write pamphlets and their main theme was an attack on the monopoly of the London City Fathers, but they had none of the vigour and determination of the Tory campaign. Eventually, the Bill was dropped.

The next step in the development of British pressure group propaganda was covered by the career of John Wilkes, a politician was a remarkable grasp of the uses of media. It was a period of slowly rising readership — sales of newspapers rose from around 35,000 a day in 1753 to around 90,000 a day in 1792, and with Coffee House readership the number of readers per copy was probably much higher than in the present day. The climax of Wilkes' career came with his Issue No. 45 of the *North Briton* in 1763 in which he attacked the royal policy. He was arrested and then proceeded to exploit the story of his own martyrdom and ultimate triumph against authority. His output of exciting stories about his in-and-out of Parliament career and about serious issues was a masterly pre-planned programme for raising circulation of the *North Briton* and maintaining public excitement. Sales rose to 60,000, a huge figure for the period. He was also one of the first British politicians to exploit public meetings, and to set up an organisation structure for his pressure group with paid officals. This was the Bill or Rights Society. He also made use of visual aids such as placards and posters.

The other outstanding British propagandist of this period was undoubtedly John Wesley. Wesley, who up to his second seeing of the light in 1738, had been a relative failure as a preacher, found a new talent in himself for creating high emotional tension in his audience by vigorous use of fire and brimstone. As he says in his journal, 'While I was speaking one before me dropped down as dead and presently a second and a third in violent agonies'. Wesley's adoption of these emotive techniques was to begin with subsconscious and in the age old tradition of prophesy, speaking direct from God, or tongues as it was often called. But soon, it became method. He says again in his journal 'I suited my discourse to my audience'. He noticed them tremble and quake. He was, now, consciously exploiting for, as he saw them, totally proper ends, namely, the enthusiastic, uninhibited, direct from God highly emotive technique of preaching to audiences, for whom, this was totally credible and who therefore were deeply affected. Preaching something like fifteen sermons a week he proceeded to use his gift for fifty years to achieve the ends he set for himself. The first of these was, rapid conversion of as many as possible. The conversion had to be reinforced and the convert used himself to convert others. First, in order to achieve the rapid conversions, Wesley would deliver his emotional assault, accusations of sin, threat of everlasting damnation, disrupting the attitude patterns of his audience, bewildering and shattering them. Then he would offer them an escape, rescue from hellfire, salvation in return for repentance. At this point in his sermon, he would change tack, using tenderness and love to reinforce his message instead of fear. Many of the characteristics of this performance bear a close resemblance to the brainwashing techniques developed after Pavlov. Although, at the same time, they fitted closely with the tradition of enthusiastic preaching from St. Paul onwards; acute emotional attack to weaken the subject followed by sudden offer of hope and salvation. Wesley noted that often those who disliked him most and resisted conversion longest were in the end converted most suddenly, (as on the road to Damascus) and most permanently. Propaganda techniques were being used, therefore, not to achieve a rational change of attitude but an emotional experience, a seeing of the light, in which the propagandist appeared to be a mere tool for some greater force.

But Wesley knew also, that the sudden conversion was not enough for a lasting change of attitude. It had to be followed up by regular reinforcement. Methodist classes limited in numbers to twelve were held once a week under class leaders. Discussions were secret. Members were encouraged to confess their deviations. Often the class leader would visit the members at home in between classes. Those who did not keep up were expelled. Indeed the whole cellular system of Methodism has a lot of the neatness and dedication of Lenin and Loyola.

The other great propaganda asset of Methodism was its use of music. Both John and Charles Wesley produced superb hymns; from *Before Jehovah's awful throne* by John to *Gentle Jesus meek and mild* by Charles. The emotive power of such superb music was and is enormous. Few other organisations have used music for propaganda purposes so effectively. Finally, Wesley made use of cheap printing techniques to reprint religious books on a large scale.

We turn now to the growing stream of political writings which formed the background to the American and French Revolutions. Richard Price's *On Civil Liberty* of 1776 sold 60,000 in hard back and 120,000 unbound. Similar success greeted Burgh's *Political Disquisitions,* Cartwright's *Take Your Choice* and Tom Paine's *Rights of Man* and *Common Sense.* There was a remarkably large audience for serious and rationally argued treatises on the human freedoms and the emergent philosophies of democracy.

In the American colonies there had been a steady development of newspapers after 1740, often full of genuine news because they were founded by post-masters who had good access to it, or by dissident printers such as the Franklin family who made a point of getting it. Besides rebellion was good for circulation and the halfpenny London Stamp Act made it essential economically for printers to risk all, in the hope of good sales. As one paper after another was closed down by the authorities and restarted under a new name, the last issue of the old would appear with a heavy black border to make the most of its funeral and draw attention to the lack of freedom of the press. Significantly, the first amendment of the U.S. constitution was in favour of press freedom.

The role of the press in helping to provide a vehicle for the American rebels was considerable. It is significant that, the so-called Boston Tea Party was a public relations exercise planned in the offices of the Boston Gazette by Samuel Adams; it was the classic ploy by which a small country makes a big one lose its temper and put itself publicly in the wrong. The incident, like the Boston massacre, then exploited to the full, publicised on broadsheets, including a picture by Paul Revere, with black border and coffin drawings, to accentuate the element of martyrdom. Meanwhile, Committees of Correspondence were formed which became the organisational propaganda basis for the Revolution, with James Otto providing considerable inspiration. Each event in the build-up to the *Declaration of Independence,* received careful pre-planned publicity from the group of media-conscious men who were organising it. For instance, the famous stage coach dash to the capital, Paul Revere the illustrator, the slogan 'Liberty or Death'.

In the war, which followed, the Americans used the propaganda advantage of controlling most of the media. The tiny skirmish of Lexington in 1776 was turned into a dramatic victory and the image of the colonists as sharp-shooters was eagerly fostered at a time when their military organisation was very poor.

Three men stand out as exceptional publicists; Washington, Jefferson and Benjamin Franklin. Washington organised readings to his troops from Paine's *American Crisis;* spared time to help organise special appeals to the French Canadians, the Indian Tribes, to Irish and German soldiers in the British army, who might desert. He practised strategic deception regularly to upset the British generals. Jefferson was a most ingenious propagandist, his *Declaration* being one of the great propaganda pamphlets of all time. It contained a clever, personalised, much repeated attack on George III. The distribution of the *Declaration,* through the network of the Committees of Correspondence and the press was most impressive and efficient. Thirdly, Franklin organised a masterly pro-American campaign in France helped secretly by the French Government-run newspaper, *Affaire,* the opposite number to the British financed *Courier de L'Europe,* published in Holland. Franklin was pictured on medallions, statuettes, prints, handkerchiefs and snuff boxes, published *The Sale of Hessians,* on the British press gangs in Germany, also *To the good people of Ireland,* as well as a fake issue of the *Boston Independent,* in which the British boasted of scalp hunting.

Once established the image projection of the new American government was fairly low key. The constitution itself was potentially a very fine propaganda document, but the overall tone was now fairly conservative. Washington himself was cultivating quite a Hanoverian image as head of state, insisting on outriders in the presidential procession, allowing no one to sit in his presence and no one to shake his hand. Meanwhile a massive propaganda war developed between the pro- and anti-Jacobins in the United States, as the new country slowly felt its way towards an image of its own. Ultimately the greatest propaganda weapon of the Americans came to be their commercial success and the huge output of basically escapist media which this success made possible. The actual image of liberty was one really created for them by the English and French Radicals. After all, it was the French who built the Statue of Liberty.

Turning now to the French Revolution we find that we are provided with a whole succession of political movements each with a remarkably sophisticated propaganda repertoire. Indeed the French revolutionary period offers more examples of cybernetic skill of different kinds than any period between Augustus and Hitler. Perhaps, this is largely a reflection of the French attempt to establish a totally new method of government, a totally new religion and at times a totally new way of life. The greater the attitude change required, the greater the

G

propaganda requirement. Russia and China in the twentieth century are the nearest parallels.

In 1789, the population of France was around 26 million with 600,000 in Paris. The media, as we shall see, were quite well developed for the period, and existing cybernetics were based on feudal law, catholicism and the image of the *Roi Soleil*, which had been fostered for Louis XIV by Charles le Brun, and the court of Versailles. Thereafter, in spite of censorship ,there had developed the highly intellectual propaganda background created by a group known as the Encyclopedists. Diderot's *Encyclopedia* was in itself a work of propaganda for new ideas, including significantly a realisation of the need for propaganda to achieve any change in society — notably propaganda by art, not words. The circulation of these works was very low, sometimes under a thousand sales — but Wade has shown the steady diffusion of the ideas of the philosopher over the period. The anti-clerical side of Voltaire's writing in particular had wider appeal.

The new ideas were played with the French aristocracy in the 'parlements', concerned as they were with reducing the King's power but not of course their own, and they produced the *Grand Remonstrance* of 1753 which sold 20,000 copies in three weeks. By 1788, helped by a further influx of ideas from America, pamphlets were appearing at the rate of twenty five per week, getting steadily more radical, calling for the end of privilege and the introduction of universal suffrage. Perhaps the greatest of these was Sieyes' *Qu'est ce que le Tiers Etat?* The new hunger for reading reached its climax in 1789, when in fact, sixty new newspapers were started.

During this preparatory period a considerable amount of propaganda skill was being developed on a more superficial level in government and finance. It is not insignificant that Necker, one of the last of the Bourbon Prime Ministers to make any real attempt to avoid a revolution, was a Swiss banker with a very sharp eye for financial public relations. He had campaigned for corn laws, for taxation of privileged classes instead of borrowing, he was the first to publish the French budget and when he resigned he made himself a martyr with the press over the rejection of his suggested reforms. There were others, also able to see the advantages of manipulation through the press; professional journalists ready to spread false

news to affect stock market values, probably the same men,
who later on, were to create panics about food shortages and
war during the Revolution, particularly the panic at the time
of the Estates General that 20,000 brigands were mustering
outside Paris. Later, the rumours of aristocratic counter-plots
made good circulation builders. To a large extent, we do not
know the truth, but we can deduce that excitements were good
business as far as the numerous newspaper proprietors were
concerned.

During the exciting meeting of the Estates General in 1789
we see developing very rapidly the semiology of the French
Revolution. In May, pamphlets were appearing at the rate of
a hundred per month; in June three hundred. The image of
the Bastille, as a symbol of oppression, packed with prisoners
was created; in fact, it was almost empty, so that its destruction
became a symbolic act of immense importance. The national
cockade; red, blue the colour of Paris and white the colour
of the Bourbons became the corporate identity of the Revolution,
to which, were later added, the Phrygian cap, the level as a
symbol of equality, the Fasces for fraternity and the oak tree
or a female figure for liberty; the club and the eye also appeared.
The Bonnet Rouge itself, was used on flag poles, church steeples,
placards, fans, watches, crockery, buttons, rings and ear-rings.
The tricolour sash was almost as common. This was one of the
most rapid and thorough spreads of a new corporate identity,
by spontaneous adoption, in all history. It helps perhaps to
account for the early quality of crowd control in the revolution.
Rudé describes the rapid development of crowd manipulation;
sounding the tocsin, fireworks, burning of effigies and hostile
tracts, processions and chanting of 'Vive le tiers état'. The
crowd was therefore turned into a weapon of the Revolution,
one which eventually got out of control, but, which was more
excited in a planned way than almost ever before. As the
abolition of feudalism proceded, so a considerable amount of
destructive hysteria was unleashed; traditional attitudes were
shaken and the population was even more susceptible to new
forms of propaganda and leadership. The tricolour and Bonnet
Rouge gave the crowd cohesion and identity, the fires and
chanting heightened its emotion — the *tutoiement* and common
form of address, Citoyen, moulded it together and its was an
instrument for use — good or ill.

Meanwhile, the Revolution had created its first hero figure, Lafayette, general of the new National Guard. In 1790, on the first anniversary of the Tennis Court Oath, we see the first effort by the new leaders at cybernetic rituals; replacing old pomp and circumstance with new. There were bronze tablets, busts of Rousseau and Franklin, waitresses dressed as patriotic nymphs, speeches by Danton and Robespierre, deputies crowned with oak leaves and a model of the Bastille which was ceremoniously smashed to pieces by members of the National Guard. Liberty was symbolised by a baby and a tree. This sort of spectacle, which became more frequent, especially when Robespierre used it to project his new religion, was the cybernetic attempt to exploit the crowd interest which the earlier excitement had created. There was a touch of 'bread and circuses', particularly when the guillotine itself, became part of the regular diet of spectacle.

In this period, there followed contributions from a series of gifted men, each in his own right an able and sometimes even innovatory propagandist. The first was Marat. Marat made two main contributions; on the one hand he was the first real mob journalist. A former doctor of doubtful qualifications he took over a Royalist press and founded the *Ami du Peuple,* with a new style of popular journalism, and within six weeks of the fall of the Bastille was campaigning for the end of the Royal veto at a time when the Assembly wanted to retain it. One particular feature of the *Ami du Peuple* was its use of correspondence columns to allow fairly extreme views to be stated; a useful ruse, which later became more widely exploited.

The other great feature of Marat's brief career was the organisation of the Popular and Fraternal Societies in 1790-91 as offshoots of the Cordeliers Club to spread Rousseau-type republicanism to the illiterate classes. Overall, he was a propagandist capable of thinking in terms of both literate and non-literate classes. It is probable that his murder cut short one of the most intelligent efforts to project republicanism to the mass of the population.

The next interesting propagandist was more of an opportunist and politician — Mirabeau, a swash-buckling publicist, who used his own newspaper to publish the States General Reports. Otherwise, his use of obscenity in his pamphlets, to attract attention or excite, was most significant in terms of propaganda technique. However, it was not sufficient for him to achieve any long term impact for his constitutional ideas.

Turning thirdly, to Robespierre, we have perhaps the most interesting of the propagandists. He, too, founded and wrote his own newspaper, *Le Defenseur de la Constitution.* He was committed to the development in France of a missionary hierarchy of the new ideals and way of life, 'Liberté et Egalité' or 'Salut et Fraternité' (it should be noted that the slogan, a superb one, 'Liberté Egalité Fraternité,' was not adopted officially in France until the 1848 revolution). Robespierre stated that he wanted the French to be armed missionaries, and he developed the Jacobin Club as an élitist cellular propaganda organisation with all the classic features we have seen used by Paul, Loyola, Wesley, and later Lenin. It was a tight-knit organisation with excellent discipline; it had its entry ritual; its test of members' orthodoxy; its own style of haircut and dress; its internal purges; its public confessions of deviation and its show trials. Not content merely with cybernetic efficiency, good control of the press, and a clearcut corporate identity, Robespierre and the Jacobin Club also wanted to appeal to the emotional side of the population; to combat the Church with their own mysticism. God was replaced by the Supreme Being, for whom an incredibly elaborate festival was organised by Robespierre, with the help of the painter David as master of pageantry. The new religion was then given its own ritual, prayers, hymns, altars, purification rites and feasts, potentially, perhaps quite a powerful combination with republicanism, but never given much of a chance to penetrate, because of the war.

Two more propagandist journalists deserve mention. Brissot was a former financial reporter of the Necker period, who had produced pamphlets against Marie-Antoinette, deliberately so provocative that they would all be bought up by the police; a good piece of business thinking. He, then, found himself a role as the great propagandist of the war period, founding his paper *Patriote Francais,* organising war demonstrations on behalf of the Girondin party with the slogan 'the war of the peoples against the Kings.' During the difficult periods of the war he resorted to the now standard ploy of keeping the people angry by means of plot scares; plots by the Austrians, or plots to save Marie-Antoinette. At the same time, he aimed on the international front to assist the French army by publishing seditious propaganda in front of it. He wrote to General Dumouriez saying, 'carry pamphlets in German on your bayonet'. Just to what extent one can talk in terms of a planned propaganda campaign across Europe, is hard to say. The idea of the Club de Propagande was probably a piece of propaganda created by their opponents. But certainly, it was in the interests of the Girondins, that the radical press throughout Europe should be encouraged to propagate French republicanism and the peoples revolt against their kings. Palmer in his *Age of Democratic Revolution* doubts if it was a deliberate campaign. But certainly there was a rapid contagion of ideas through masonic lodges, reading clubs for the joint purchase of French papers, and a remarkable growth in the printing of revolutionary texts in almost every European language.

In Belgium Tom Paine was published in Flemish and Walloon, and *Le Cosmopolite* was the new revolutionary paper. In Holland, it was *Le Batave* and they were using *Liberty, Equality, Fraternity,* as their motto as early as 1795. In Poland, there was a Jacobin type club. They wore Phrygian caps, sang translated French songs and under Kosciuszko had a flourishing revolutionary movement. In Hungary, Rumania, Serbia and other parts of the Austrian Empire again there were French newspapers specially for the region, translated songs, pamphlets and even Jacobin haircuts. In England, there was the London Corresponding Society, an organisation for the distribution of Jacobin propaganda, collecting 1d (½p) a week from each member and succeeding in selling 200,000 copies of the *Rights of Man* in 1793. Such results could not have been achieved without a considerable inspiration from Paris, some of it, perhaps, from Brissot, some, perhaps, from Lebrun, the Foreign Secretary, who also, as it so happened, was an excellent journalist. In Ireland, the *Belfast Northern Star,* published twice weekly at under 2d (1p) per copy has been called, 'one of the most significant democratic papers in English', encouraging, as it did, the development of the Orange Lodges and the revolutionary Irish poetry of Wolfe Tone.

The last of the great revolutionary newspaper propagandists was Hebert, founder of *Père Duchesne* which was subsidised by the Jacobins and is reputed at one point to have achieved a circulation of a million. This paper was more populist than any of its predecessors, more obscene than Mirabeau, more left wing than Marat. It called for government grants for the *sansculottes,* was violent and ultimately irresponsible, but formed a model for a number of imitators in Belgium, Holland and elsewhere.

The press, then, in the French Revolution was of enormous importance, helped by the very significant fact that newspapers in France were about half the price of those in London, and that, throughout Europe the illiterate were helped to enjoy their contents by the spread of various kinds of reading clubs. Many of the circulations were naturally quite small; Robespierre's paper about 2000. The *Moniteur's* figure is not known, but the *Journal de Paris* had 12,000 paid subscribers at a time when the leading British paper, *The Times,* had only 4,000. In addition to newspapers, was the massive output of books and pamphlets, particularly Rousseau and Tom Paine. It is interesting that the first signs of genuine counter-attack in Britain were not Burke's *Reflections* which itself sold twelve editions, but the more mass appeal of Hannah More's cheap Repository Tracts, subsidised by the Duke of Gloucester in 1795 and at 1d (½p) each selling something like two million copies. This was a more real sign of early exploitation of the beginnings of working class literacy in Britain.

Having looked at the printed medium in the French Revolution in some depth, there are three other media: painting, theatre and music.

In painting, David, who had been called in by the Jacobin Club to paint the Tennis Court Oath, must rank as one of the greatest propagandist painters of all time, no less because he was equally effective for Napoleon later. As a Jacobin deputy David produced his famous *Death of Marat* and *Le Peletier.* He was briefed by the Assembly's Committee of Public Instruction, the beginnings of a propaganda ministry, to project 'la vertu' and in due course the Convention appointed a jury to vet revolutionary painting. Helped by, or in spite of, such patronage David and other painters such as Jeaurat, Gericault, with his *Ossian receives the generals of the Republic in Walhalla* and Gros, produced a style of romanticised classicism which gave both the Revolutionary and Napoleonic periods artistic panache. At the same time, David was the Jacobin pageant master, just as the architect Speer was later to help create spectacles for Hitler. The famous Fête of 10th August cost 1,200,000 livres and included torchlight processions, arches, Bastille guns, salvoes and a cardboard figure of Atheism. Not only did the Revolution have its basic graphic themes and its painting, but every other aspect of visual style was affected. In architecture, there was the love of classical styles; triumphal arches, statues, laurel wreaths, the redecorated Pantheon with its republican murals and the Temple of the Revolution — la Madeleine. Perhaps no political movement has ever established so rapidly such a new and stylish visual imagery to balance the intellectual influence it exercised through print.

Theatre, too, played its part. It was particularly encouraged by Robespierre and of course there was a good deal of theatre in his rituals and spectacles.

Finally, there was music — the great international songs of the Revolution. *Ca Ira* was immensely popular throughout Europe and translated into most of its languages — from Irish to Hungarian. The great war anthem, Marseillaise was also a piece of musical propaganda of real genius. Even Thermidore had its theme tune, *La reveil du Peuple*. The founding of the National Conservatory of Music in 1795 endorsed the Revolution's sponsorship of musical propaganda. Indeed, the flare with which music, art and literature came together with organisational skill for propaganda planning and agitation make the French Revolution for all its failures a milestone in the history of cybernetics. Although the political effectiveness was limited in the short term, image penetration was very considerable and the ideas of the Revolution were never far below the surface in Europe throughout the nineteenth century.

The particularly remarkable thing about propaganda in the French Revolution, was the consciousness of the need for social cybernetics, an awareness that traditional forms of authority had been undermined and that new myths were needed. As Britt and and Varenne suggested, in 1794, they needed *d'inspirer l'amour des vertus civiles'*. Perhaps what they underestimated was the time that it takes even for a highly imaginative propaganda campaign such as they had, to achieve real penetration. They ran out of time before the ideas had really taken root.

Napoleon must rank with Caesar and Hitler as one of the great single propagandists of all time. Brilliant as he was as a soldier and political opportunist, it was by deliberately creating an image that he gained the power to dominate Europe for fifteen years, and for Bonapartism to survive long after his death. At the same time, it must be acknowledged that the propaganda tools, which he used, had nearly all been developed or used successfully under the Revolution.

Bonaparte's awareness of the power of propaganda came early on. As a Jacobin army officer he obtained the help of an Italian friend, Salucetti to write a pamphlet called *Souper de Beaucare,* which put over the case for Marseilles surrendering to the Jacobin army without a fight in 1793. Thereafter, he always recognised the importance of making sure that his military successes were exaggerated and his failures blamed on others. He wrote an account of Marengo, which gave him sole credit for a brilliant victory, by getting in first to the media before his opposite number Moreau, who had really won a more substantial battle at Hohenlinden. He also published his *Bulletin of the Army of Reserve,* his equivalent to Caesar's *Gallic War.* There were those delightful set pieces like his crossing of St. Bernard's Pass, reading Livy as he negotiated frozen torrents. Always he cultivated the 'whiff of grapeshot' image, swash-buckling, outwitting the enemy, which he often did, everything in heroic mould. His defeats were played down. Copenhagen, he distorted, Aboukir he blamed on Bruys, Trafalgar on Villeneuve and Waterloo on Ney. This deliberately cultivated image of the dashing commander, who was also popular with his men, was crucial to his entire career, and while based on genuine military ability of a very high order, it hid the deficiencies.

Napoleon's second main early propaganda technique was the old revolutionary one in which Brissot had specialised — the half-invented plot. By advertising terrorist conspiracies, real or false, of either Jacobin or Royalist origin, he prepared the population to accept dictatorship. Later, he encouraged the exaggerated reports of the Cadoudal conspiracy to convert his title of First Consul to Emperor.

Once in power, Napoleon was able to use a wider range of cybernetic techniques. He had begun to create the Bonaparte legend and now also began to project the visual Napoleonic image. The romantic Byronic profile was created by David, like Alexander the Great, heroic on his charger, the romantic folk-hero in the Ossianic mould; his hair, face, clothes and style were created to fit his role and by 1802 his head was appearing on coins, medals, statues and paintings. There was the classic Napoleon picture with his eagles and triumphs, the followers painted by Gericault in works such as his *1812 Officier de Chasseur de la Garde* or *Ossian receiving the generals of the Republic in Walhalla,* an entire mythology of glorified militarism, the concept of 'mon aigle' or 'soldats, il vous suffira de dirè, j'étais à la battaile de l'Austerlitz . . . . pour que l'on responde Voila un brave'. This idolisation of 'la gloiré' was the climax of a nationalist propaganda campaign that dated back to Brissot, where the rights of man were much less important than the willingness of man to sacrifice his life for the sake of nation or emperor. Napoleon said somewhat cynically that 'history is a myth which people choose to believe'. He applied this principle, ruthlessly, in order to foster a self-denial ethic in his Empire.

Not only did David and the other painters help create the new myth — David's huge picture of the imperial coronation was done with as much feeling as the same painter's *Tennis Court Oath,* a new style with the revolution rounded it off with the Empire and were used, but other forms of art, which had begun to develop ruthlessly, in order to foster a self-denial ethic in his Empire. The architecture, decor and fashion were all three consciously imperial — imitated from a mixture of the great Empires of the past: Roman, Etruscan and Egyptian. Triumphal arches and victory columns, everything was on the grand scale in the massive public works, put in hand in Paris, between 1804 and 1813.

Once in power, Napoleon had complete control of the press and used it to advantage. As he said, 'three hostile newspapers are more to be feared than a thousand bayonets'. So hostile newspapers were suppressed. In 1800 he closed down 60 out of 73 French papers and within a year removed another four. The *Moniteur* became the official government paper under Marat and was distributed free to the army. Censorship was intensified. "If I had a free press I wouldn't last more than three months", said Napoleon. He set up the *Direction General de l'Imprimerie et de la Librairie* to take responsibility for all cultural life in 1810. By now, there were only four papers left. The *Mercure de la France* had been suppressed in 1807 because of an anti-government article by the poet Chateaubriand, who had earlier written in favour of Napoleon, particularly after the Concordat with the Pope.

There was also his use of coins with mottoes such as *Union et Force* in 1800; his portrait appeared from 1802 onwards with *Republique Francaise* on one side till 1809 when the legend became *Napoleon Empereur.*

Napoleon was fully aware of the value of institutional propaganda — the Concordat with the Papacy allowed him to use the parish clergy for pulpit propaganda on his behalf — they always sang a *Te Deum* for his victories — so that he had the huge value of the established hierarchy behind him. In addition he realised the importance of law as a tool of communication. His code, all in one book, easily translated into other languages, was a neat way of projecting the more imperially useful aspects of the revolution to other European countries.

Finally, we may look briefly at Napoleon's military and diplomatic propaganda. We have already seen his use of leaflets in front of the armies and his somewhat hypocritical projection of French liberty in countries such as Italy which had previously been so totally subjected that even a hint of liberalism was welcome. More subtle, was the production under Talleyrand, of an English newspaper, the *Argus,* edited by Lewis Goldsmith and distributed in the West Indies and to British prisoners of war in places like Verdun. Later Goldsmith edited the *British Monitor* before finally changing sides and writing French propaganda for the British.

In total, therefore, propaganda played an unusually important role in the career of Napoleon. While he did not contribute much in the way of new techniques, other than perhaps the byronicisation of military glory, he had a particularly acute awareness of the possibilities and a remarkable grasp of all the available techniques. Perhaps his one great novelty was the plebiscite, the idea of a popular vote on an issue where the result was a foregone conclusion and then publicising the figures. It was a technique copied in particular by his nephew Napoleon III and of course Hitler. Before leaving Napoleonic propaganda, we should look briefly at its posthumous resurrection, as this in itself shows that the myth was strong enough to survive the reality of several humiliating defeats. Certainly it was kept alive by a number of able writers; Victor Hugo for one with his *Ode à la Colonne* and Beranger with his popular lyrics. In 1849 there appeared a whole new Napoleon cult; prints, medals, brooches, *image d'Epinal* cut-outs of Napoleon and his marshalls, and endless commercial souvenirs that were good business and of sufficient political power to help restore the dynasty in the name of Napoleon III.

Perhaps the sad part of this period of brilliant propaganda development was that it was easier to project the image of liberalism than to make the idea work. The techniques for mass motivation developed in the French Revolution for liberal purposes were soon misused for imperial objectives. The new emperors and dictators were able to give empire building a new lease of life by exploiting new nationalist images. Mass conscription was first practised by Carnot in 1797. Mass motivation of armies began seriously at about the same time.

NINETEENTH-CENTURY PROPAGANDA

The nineteenth century was essentially a period of technological improvement rather than new ideas in the field of cybernetics. The penetration of print certainly increased dramatically. On the one hand, the development of rotary printing in the 1840's made larger circulations possible. Railway transport, machine type-setting, and photo-engraving, all contributed. The steady increase in literacy in western Europe did the rest. The 1830's in fact saw the appearance of the first genuinely proletarian print media and although it was not recognised as such, the publication of the Communist Manifesto in 1848 introduced what was to be probably the most potent propaganda pamphlet since the New Testament. While it was not accompanied by any of the other facets of a propaganda organisation which might have made it more successful in its own time, it did have a certain apocalyptic appeal which underlined its potential. The vision of the underdog, the have-nots taking over from the millennium of the bourgeois, the workers losing their chains, had the same kind of promise that Christianity had made to the underdogs of the Roman Empire.

The period 1830 - 1848 was one then of media expansion and a new penetration of revolutionary ideas in many countries to a lower social level than before, but not of any major propaganda upheavals. The revolutionary movements did not succeed in grasping sufficient of the other available cybernetic techniques to achieve lasting political success.

Chartism, in England for example, had some of the ingredients, but in media terms never seemed to get beyond the provincial. It was economically possible for O'Connor to run the *Northern Star and Leeds and General Advertiser* costing 4½d (1½p) as a local paper in Yorkshire, but not yet to distribute a mass circulation daily paper nationally. There were plenty of other local papers with Chartist leanings and there were a number of untaxed weeklies in the tradition of Cobbett's *Register* which at times between 1802 and 1835 topped the 60,000 mark with its anti-Jacobin line. For instance, there were Wooler's *Black Dwarf* and Horne's *Reformist Register,* both projecting a very radical point of view. Chartism made use of other media too; there were the Grand Demonstrations such as the one in Glasgow in 1838 where there were 43 bands, 300 banners, 70 unions and 200,000 people in a mile long procession. The petition for the charter itself was an impressive publicity performance, three miles long with half a million signatures taken to Westminster on a decorated cart. There were exciting slogans such as 'Equal representation or Death,' and Chartist hymns, slopshop propaganda and Mechanics Institutes for the spread of ideas to the semi-literate. But for all this ability to use media O'Connor and his colleagues lacked the consistent organisational power to keep up an effective long-term campaign.

A contemporary who had more success in a limited field and provides a classic example of a well organised propaganda pressure group is Cobden and the Anti-Corn Law League. This organisation had many of the facets of a modern political party; its own newspaper, its full-time executives, its fund-raising bazaars, its banners, badges and even its famous free trade halls. A more élitist, but also successful approach to achieving specific objectives through propaganda and pressure groups was operated by men such as Chadwick on Public Health, Wilberforce on Abolition, and Shaftesbury on Child Labour.

Elsewhere in Europe there were flickerings of propaganda excitement. Metternich, as he departed from the political scene in Vienna commented wryly, 'that the power of the free press was a scourge unknown in the world before the last half of the eighteenth century'. There were sufficient outbursts of liberal or national feeling to topple men like him from time to time, but not to make adequate use of the initial success. The Romantics, who had earlier made some contribution to Napoleon's image, now made their contribution, particularly for Greek and Polish liberation — Byron's poetry and Delacroix's painting, but again it was not a sustained effort. In France, St Simon and Proudhon were exciting pamphleteers. In Germany, a group of gifted writers were beginning to help project a new liberal nationalist German image; Korner and Arndt had begun the tradition of resistance song writing. There was the cult of old symbols, national dress, folk-lore and a new Teutonic image for the German people. *Wacht am Rhein* was composed in 1840 and Fichte developed his Urvolk ideas, but all this was part of a slow attitude development process, not backed up by sufficient organisational effort for any short term political success, lying dormant, slowly simmering, ready to erupt under Kaiser Wilhelm II and later Hitler.

In Italy, perhaps, more concrete results were achieved by propagandists than anywhere in Europe in the nineteenth century. All three of the protagonists in the struggle for Italian reunification were able propagandists; Cavour was a former journalist, ex-editor of the *Risorgimento;* Mazzini was a professional pamphleteer of outstanding brilliance, and Garibaldi, with his thousand red-shirts, his special anthem and his swashbuckling image, projected himself with all the requirements for hero worship. Mazzini, as the theorist of the three, showed a particular understanding of cybernetics. He wrote 'one must always preach the necessity of insurrection and when it succeeds provide the principles of national education'. He understood both the full implications of trying to displace old attitudes and create new ones in their place, and also the need for continued motivation even when first political goals had been reached.

Given the spasmodic but steadily spreading projection of liberal, socialist and nationalist ideas in the nineteenth century, we turn to one other concept, which showed a sudden revival towards the end of the century and one which was to have drastic results — imperialism. We have seen the idolisation of empire and glory fostered by Brissot and Napoleon. Late nineteenth century imperialism bore some relation to it. It was partly attributable to the geographic fact of newly discovered lands available for the creation of empires. But as the division of Africa, and other undeveloped areas, among the great powers proceeded, so they developed propaganda to justify themselves and motivate their peoples. Thus, this was likely to make the movement perpetuate itself beyond the natural point of completion, creating the jingoistic attitudes which were largely responsible for the First World War.

In Britain, there was the almost accidental development of a code of imperial cybernetics, geared without a great deal of planning to the psychological needs of a class ruling 320 million people and to a lesser extent the needs of the actual subjects. Large lithographs of the Great White Queen hung not only in every British home but also in most Indian and Ceylonese middle class homes. The plumes and steel of the Royal Horse Guards, the salaams to the Queen Empress, the throng of princes attending the Delhi Durba, the three new knightly orders, these were all part of the spectacle which the British slowly created to suit their imperial role and project their image.

The British churches, too, played their part in imperial cybernetics, fielding at one point as many as 360 missions with 12,000 missionaries. They achieved a total conversion of something like ten million new christians, who thus had a potentially greater loyalty to Britain.

In so far as this propaganda had any official origin in the governmental sense, it was Disraeli who came nearest to a political articulation of the imperial image. He had already had some success as a propagandist novelist with *Sybil*. His 'Empire and Liberty' slogan, his change of Victoria's title to Empress were all part of his encouragement of the jingoistic image.

Thereafter, we can see it appearing in all forms of art. Statues of an imperial Victoria stood in almost every colonial capital, Lady Butler's paintings captured the military self-effacing ethic — *Rorke's Drift, Roll Call, Steady the Fifes and Drums,* and *Floreat Etona* — a new front of enlightened militarism. In music, there was Elgar's *Caractacus,* and *Land of Hope and Glory.* In architecture, there was the new Gothic imperial of George Gilbert Scott, the Ottowa Parliament buildings and the flurry of Gothic cathedrals in Sydney and Calcutta, or the Gothic palace of the White Rajahs of Sarawak.

On the literary side Kipling, above all, projected the imperial message; his *Recessional* was to be printed in *The Times,* his novels crowned the motivation of the Indian Army and Civil Service, the classic imperial career structure. Even more extreme, were writers such as G. A. Henty with *By Sheer Pluck,* the *Union Jack Magazine;* the poet laureate Alfred Austin produced a eulogy of the Jamieson raid; Rider Haggard's *She* was turned into the new medium, film and in 1897 this was the first film to be shown in Ceylon. Angela Brazil's *A Patriotic Schoolgirl,* was typical of the best-selling attitude-formers for middle class teenage girls. Overall the image of the British carrying the white man's burden; Gordon of Khartoum, Raffles, Pomp and Circumstance, the Thin Red Line, were all the keys to cybernetic motivation for controlling the Empire, but at the same time were inevitably the foundation for motivating imperial war if ever the Empire should be seriously threatened. In Britain, and as we shall see elsewhere in Europe, the cyberntics of one era had an almost inevitable by-product in the next.

In France we see the development of a very similar, equally unplanned jingoistic propaganda scheme. The Foreign Legion was idealised, glory and warfare under a tropical sun were projected as the ideal ethic. Marianne, the female personification of France, was usually seen armed and in the last quarter of the century art and writing projected chauvinistic war idolatry, particularly in the period leading up to the Alsace War of 1899. That it was out of control, is shown by the unpleasant anti-semitic overtones of papers like *Anti-Juif;* the attitude it represented and the Dreyfus affair.

In Germany too, there was idolisation of the military. Since Wagner had composed his ostentatious *Kaisermarsch* in the excitement of victory and reunification in 1871, the Germans naturally had a sudden feeling of their own strength. Bismarck had restrained this, but the new hereditary warlord, Kaiser Wilhelm II, while he paid lip-service to pacifism was tempted by ambition and obsessed with the 'knight in shining armour' image. A commentator, on seeing his new portrait said 'That is not a portrait, but a declaration of war.' He adopted a swash-buckling posture and his speeches tended to be inflammatory. At the time of the Boxer rebellion in China he was talking of 'Huns standing together against the savage foe', and briefing a tame artist to draw 'the yellow peril' for popular consumption. The whole new Prussian image: spiked helmets, shin-length great-coats, monocles and everywhere the German eagle, was dedicated to military glory and the Reich.

The Kaiser was particularly eloquent on naval matters and the image rivalry of the two great fleets of Dreadnoughts (an emotive name in itself), which in effect were never to have a proper battle with each other, was more important than any real naval competition. The rivalry of images, the importance of being seen to be the biggest, most powerful, meant that the naval rivalry of the two nations was partly a peacock propaganda exercise, so that a challenge had to mean war. It was significant that the first propaganda film known to have been made in Germany was *Life in the German Navy* which was specially filmed on the Kaiser's orders.

It would be rash to suggest that propaganda caused the Great War; what we can say is that the inculcation of militaristic attitudes in France, Britain, Germany and Russia, was so deep that these nations were highly likely to join in a war if their image was threatened, and the glorification of war made the whole thing more likely. For the struggling Russian government, in particular, war was really only a propaganda tool. They had more than enough territory to cope with, but were always desperate for a foreign victory to restore their image at home and re-enthuse their people. It was Russia's propaganda orientated interest in Serbia, which led to the first stages of the war.

Another example of the media fanning militarism was the contribution of the Hearst newspaper empire to exciting the Americans about Cuba in 1899 — many of the stories used were largely untrue, but good for circulation and encouraged the idea of war. Just as, in his calculating way, Bismarck deliberately leaked a shortened text of the Ems telegram to the French and German press, knowing that their desire to excite would do the rest, so Kaiser Wilhelm II watched his own arrogant postures mirrored in his press and postured the more.

In Japan, xenophobia became an obsession. The propaganda by the ruling class called for resistance to all things foreign and this was so well promoted by the symbolic use of the Emperor from 1867 onwards and the Imperial Rescript of 1890 which demanded Spartan type self-sacrifice, that from a defence theme it became an obsession to attack. The propaganda theme was out of control. The result was ultimately disastrous.

These examples show how the art and literature which provides the ethos for an expanding country often creates a much less comfortable emotional posture for the generation which follows.

H

LENIN AND COMMUNISM

Communism, as a communicable idea, was lucky in having two great propagandists, each working fifty years apart and in different countries. Marx was the great theoretical propagandist and Lenin the great administrative one. We have already noted that Marx was not really a practical communicator, but his writings did embody considerable appeal; the apocalyptic doom of the rich and the earthly salvation of the poor; the millennial end of capitalism. The mystic inevitability of everything he suggested had the appeal of an Old Testament prophet and his promise was a good one. Phrases like 'Workers of the world unite, you have nothing to lose but your chains', had huge emotive power, even in translation. Like Marx, Lenin was rather a one-sided propagandist, but provided Communism with the sort of communication infra-structure that dovetailed with Marx's revelation. Russia was of course vast, with a high level of illiteracy, fairly effective censorship, and conventional media were weak. But it did have the habit of receptivity to images. McLuhan writes, 'The Russians had only to adapt their tradition of the Easter Ikon and image building to the new electric media in order to be aggressively effective in the modern world of information'. Tsarist propaganda in the late nineteenth century consisted mainly of vain efforts to win wars, Cossack cavalry charges to inspire terror, patriotic sermons by the orthodox clergy and a display of ikons. Artistic effort was wasted from a media point of view on the introverted decoration of Fabergé eggs and other trinkets. The Tsars felt they hardly needed to use cybernetic skills on their people, because it ought to be devoted to them. Significantly, the Tsarist government ran out of poster glue in Petrograd in 1917, so that it was harder than ever to state its case at the time when it was most needed.

On the liberal and socialist side propaganda, up to the time of Lenin, tended to consist mainly of isolated acts of terrorism, peasant missionaries and martyrs, anarchists and intellectuals appealing to limited audiences. Lenin's gifts of single-minded dedication and administration resulted in a consistent, longer term campaign of newspaper propaganda deliberately aimed at potential activists with cellular follow-up. From 1894 onwards, he was helping to organise the printing of Marxist text books under phoney titles so that they would evade the censors. In 1900, he launched *Iskra* (The Spark). As Lenin put it, *Iskra* was to start a 'conflagration to which there is still no end'. Nevertheless, though it was perhaps one of the most important propaganda newspapers ever to be printed *Iskra* was not a brilliant or popular newspaper. Printed in Munich, financed by Strive, edited by Plekhanov, it was never easy reading; it tended to be dull and doctrinaire, intellectual rather than emotively exciting and aimed at an interested élite rather than the crowd. Much of its success was due to the indefatigable efforts of Lenin's wife Krupskaya, who organised its circulation, smuggled in from Switzerland into Russia in double-bottomed trunks. This circulation network, painstakingly built up, was to be of enormous importance as the basis of the party. The fact that the paper was passed on through such a network, to a known audience, as opposed to being sold at random, or dispersed carelessly, made it infinitely more effective. At its height, the circulation was around 40,000.

In 1902, came Lenin's brilliant pamphlet *Shto Dyelat?* (What's to be done?) which put over the concept of a cellular élite bringing about the revolution, rather than a dispersed and uncontrolled rising of the whole population. The utilisation of a dedicated minority with strict disciplne and total loyalty to communist dogma was to be one of Lenin's most consistent themes, one over which he fell out with the Mensheviks, but one which became the cornerstone of his ultimate success. The remarkable ease of the takeover of such a large country by such a small number of Bolsheviks becomes intelligible. Two other notable points about *Shto Dyelat?* are its distinction between the arts of agitation and propaganda, which was to be fundamental in Soviet cybernetic thinking, and also the fact that it was distributed through the *Iskra* circulation network—Krupskaya's great contribution.

1904 saw one of the many setbacks in Lenin's long road to power. In the party split, which resulted in the division into Mensheviks and Bolsheviks, Lenin lost control of *Iskra* to the the Mensheviks and had to start a new newspaper. This was *Vperyod* (Forward); he also helped launch another paper, *Novaya Zhisn* (New Life), with the help of money from Russian industrialists. Maxim Gorky, perhaps the most sensitive writer about Tsarist oppression, was a major contributor and the circulation soon rose to around 50,000. The fourth great paper was

Pravda (Truth) which was founded by Trotsky to combat the Menshevik *Ray. Pravda,* too, had a healthy circulation, and *Pravda of the Trenches,* a free sheet subsidised by the Germans during World War I to foster disloyalty in the Russian Army, particularly against Kerensky, was also important for a brief period.

From a propaganda point of view, the revolution of 1905 was a non-event. The Bolshevik infra-structure was not yet ready; no other consistent scheme of attitudes had penetrated adequately. Maxim Gorky's song, *At the Bottom* was the hit song of the year, but Father Gapon, the nearest to a hero figure in the Revolution was a Tsarist plant, so the Revolution was defused.

In viewing the Revolutions of 1917, it is important to remember that the first one in March was the natural death of a tired and totally unsuccessful régime, which had lost all credibility and which could neither feed nor protect its people. Neither the ikon nor the Cossack charge would any longer work. But the Revolution was not planned or created by the Bolsheviks. It was the social democratic Duma which seized power and the new Soviets who showed most signs of knowing how to use it. There was every danger that the March Revolution would be so successful that Lenin and the Bolsheviks would be superfluous and miss their opportunity for ever. Luckily, for Lenin, the Social Democrats made mistakes, the greatest of them being to attempt to continue the war. Lenin, thus, had time to reorganise his propaganda machine, with German help, and allign his cellular élite with the Soviets. The Soviets were a metric pyramid, one man representing a thousand and so on. Lenin put himself in the position of dominating Russia with a small élite, simply, by first of all dominating the Soviets. What was crucial, was that he had such a totally dedicated, dogma-trained élite ready for the purpose. So his main slogan became 'All power to the Soviets', and his main propaganda theme was very simple — to give the people the three things it wanted: food, peace and land.

Inevitably, the technique of propaganda in the hurried circumstances before and after the October Revolution was opportunistic. *Isvestia,* as the organ of the Soviets, was important. The news of Lenin's promises, particularly the all important land decree had to be transmitted by any available means and there was a drastic shortage of paper, as of most commodities, due to the war. The radio station at Tsarskoe Selo was used to speed up the spread of news to provincial centres, the earliest known contribution of radio to propaganda. Bolshevik soldiers were also used to spread the news.

In terms of themes exploited, many of them were the familiar material of revolutionary situations. First of all, there had to be a scapegoat for failures and difficulties. To start with, it was the bourgeois and the Whites, later under Stalin, the Kulaks or wealthy peasants. Then, there had to be the artificial panics to keep discipline; plots were invented or exaggerated just as they had been in the French Revolution. There followed the display of force and brutality to intimidate; the threat to lynch social revolutionaries; the use of toughs from the navy, who, in turn, had to be intimidated to prevent loss of control. Visually, to begin with, the October Revolution was unexciting; there was a triumphal arch for Lenin's arrival at Petrograd station; there were red and gold banners with Marxist devices, but for years there was neither the time or money to embellish the new régime and its image was Spartan. The Hammer and Sickle was not developed in any definite style. On the musical side, too, it was slow to get going. In October the band played the *Marseillaise* because they did not know the *Internationale*.

What was remarkable about the propaganda sense of the Bolsheviks was the speed, so soon after their coup, and skill with which they proceeded to set up an organisation for the propaganda conquest of the rest of the world. As early as 1917 a section was set up under Radek for international propaganda and a budget of two million roubles set aside for the world-wide spread of Communism. It produced a daily paper in German, called *Die Fachel,* aimed at the lower ranks of the German and Austrian armies and putting over basic Marxism. Soon it was also produced in other languages. At the same time as this activity, propaganda by the Bolshevik definition meant the long term inculcation of a system of ideas. There was also training for agitation, defined by Lenin as being the explanation and exploitation of particular issues which excite the masses. For this purpose, potential leaders from foreign countries, particularly those in the East, were invited to Moscow for training. There was a brilliant propaganda school founded at Tashkent with the specific objective of training an élite from the Indian sub-continent. Ultimately the effort with the Chinese was more successful.

Initially, the main objective of international propaganda was to stop the war, to discourage other countries from assisting the White Russians in the civil war which had developed. The slogans were 'Long Live the Third Internationale' and 'War on Great houses, peace to the Cottages', the latter borrowed from the French. Lenin used Joffe to organise an anti-Kaiser campaign in Berlin. After Versailles he wrote to him, saying 'We must publish a hundred times more'. Though propaganda across the frontier was specifically forbidden by the Treaty of Brest-Litosk it carried on, particularly against the Whites. Then the Baku Council of Propaganda launched a new paper, *Peoples of the East,* in four languages, and the Comintern, founded in 1919, was geared to fostering Marxist agitation in Europe. Bernard Shaw commented, 'The working man respects the bourgeoisie and wants to be a bourgeois: Marx never got hold of him for a moment'. This statement was certainly not true of Europe in the years immediately after the Treaty of Versailles. Communism made considerable inroads in France and Britain. This was the period of the Red Clyde. In Germany, it was strong enough for Hitler to set himself up as a plausible antidote. Perhaps the socialist alternative offered too many of the same advantages with fewer of the disadvantages. Certainly, while the Comintern created a useful reservoir of trained agitators in many countries, most Russian propaganda continued to be doctrinaire and authoritarian. Marxist exegesis tended to be dull and pedantic, and except in Russia itself, the abstract ideas were not embellished with enough myth or metaphor to catch the mass imagination. The international propaganda campaigns by Moscow against Jugoslav communism after 1948 and Maoism after 1963 tended to be formal and doctrinaire. Indeed they have been compared to the duller polemics of the Papal investiture contest.

Internally, the propaganda of the Soviet régime has been massive—rather than subtle. Their press media are still essentially dull — *Pravda* and *Isvestia* carry a barely disguised repetition of daily dogma, uninspired parables and flaccid testimonials to party loyalty. All news is properly organised by the government long before press day. In terms of efficiency of output and censorship their media are unexcelled, magazines such as

Rabotnitsa (The Female Worker), reaching a circulation of over ten million. The early revolutionary period, too, saw a massive output of good quality books for children, complete revision of all text books; indeed under Stalin most history was rewritten to establish Russian credit for major discoveries. After Gorky, most court literature was fairly uninspired; men like Sholokov were officially favoured, men like Pasternak and Solzhenitsyn strayed from the party line into disfavour.

In terms of other transmission media, radio, cinema and later television were used, though none of them, except on rare occasions cinema, with particular imagination. The *Kino-pravda* of the early days was an excitingly produced cinema news-propaganda series, and brilliant directors like Eisenstein were able to translate into artistic cinema form the intended image of the new Russia. The use of odd camera angles to magnify and dramatise the mini-revolution in Odessa in *The Battleship Potemkin* to make the audience feel involved, heralded the ability of the new medium to communicate with real power and was later imitated by Goebbels. In terms of music, there was Shostakovich to project the new revolutionary soul and composers like Khachaturian at the next level of motivation. In painting, propaganda tended to dominate, and with rather crude realism at that. Better than most were the two Gerasimovs, Alexander with his *State Stockbreeding Farm,* a delicate ikon of the new era, and Sergei with his Goya-type pictures of the war. There were also the endless heroic illustrations of Soviet success, particularly of the Stalinist period, such as Serov's recreation of the October Revolution with Stalin in a leading role. The same picture had been previously painted with less of him. In sculpture, heroic realism tended to be the order of the day, like Sergei Merkurov's *Stalin,* with its pent-up energy and almost idolatrous oversell. Finally, in architecture the same half-articulate giganticism, the massive success symbol of the original dam at Dniepropetrovsk, and the equally ostentatious Moscow Underground on whose construction Kruschev made his reputation. So art and cybernetics, in Russia, were inextricably linked.

In all, the organisation of the arts for propaganda produced a mass of workmanlike material and some works of genius. But it tended to be for home consumption, lacking credibility abroad, lacking the excitement for further mass conversion, in fact geared more to the stabilisation of the existing converts and their corporate mental security.

Lenin, as we have seen, did make a very notable contribution in that he was the first politician to plan his own political propaganda so carefully, and also to think thereafter in terms of world conquest for his ideas. Stalin, on the other hand, had more limited objectives. Apart from the cult of his own personality which Lenin had largely avoided, his propaganda was mainly mundane or negative. His elimination of the Kulaks showed some subtlety. Solzhenitsyn in the *Gulag Archipelago* comments on how the meaning of the word *Kulak,* originally a dishonest trader, was applied to all well-to-do peasants by 1930, and Stalin of course wanted rid of well-to-do peasants. The new word podkulachnik meant 'a creep'. The propaganda campaign against these peasants, as quasi - bourgeois enemies of the state, preceded their total elimination. Show trials, public confessions and intimidation were a special feature of Stalinist propaganda, but perhaps his most notable achievement in this field was his about-turn and resuscitation of the old patriotic themes to motivate his people in the darkest period of the war against Hitler.

In terms of the Communist propaganda achievement as a whole, perhaps their greatest real long term success internally has been the *Komsomol;* the concept of doctrinal training of children from a very early age; practised in Sparta, recommended by Plato and copied by Hitler. By 1972, 45% of all youths in the 15 - 26 age group were members of the *Komsomol,* having previously passed through the various junior feeding systems, which make Soviet education, politically, so effective. The *Komsomol* has it own media; over 200 million newspapers a year. With such penetration, propaganda for the older age groups becomes relatively unimportant.

Qualitatively it is difficult to judge the internal Soviet propaganda achievement — it is too close to monopoly. Internationally, it has not lived up to the huge promise of 1917-19, perhaps largely because of its lack of adaptability. Whereas Christianity, a message originally designed for the worst-off classes of society, adapted itself to attract the upper classes, Communism in theory often failed to compromise, thus failing to clinch its stronghold in countries such as Italy and Portugal in 1975-76.

HITLER AND FASCISM

Hitler shares with Julius Caesar and Napoleon Bonaparte, the distinction of not only making massive use of new methods of propaganda but also, of quite consciously and deliberately basing his entire career on planned propaganda. Goebbels, who had taken a doctorate in romantic drama and later worked as a publicity man for the Strassers, recognised the quality of Hitler's analysis of propaganda in *Mein Kampf* as:

"a carefully built up erection of statements, which whether true or false can be made to undermine quite rigidly held ideas and to construct new ones that will take their place. It would not be impossible to prove with sufficient repetition and psychological understanding of the people concerned that a square is in fact a circle. What after all are a square and a circle? They are mere words and words can be moulded until they clothe ideas in disguise".

We shall see, however, that Hitler's feelings for propaganda stretched much further than his understanding of the use of words. Before proceeding to his use of media, there are other cardinal principles which he preached in *Mein Kampf*. One should avoid abstract ideas and appeal instead to the emotions (this was where he was to score against the Marxists); one should constantly repeat a few stereotyped phrases, never be objective; in other words only put one side of the argument, criticise the enemy violently and always try to identify one special enemy.

We shall see how consistently he stuck to these principles; the constant repetition both verbal and visual, the identification and vituperation of specified scapegoats; first the Versailles Traitors, then the Communists, then the Jews. He provided one group for the Germans to look down on, another for them to look up to, the Aryan élite, himself, the new heroes of Germany, even totally artificial heroes such as Horst Wessel, the martyred hooligan. Certainly his appeal was emotional not intellectual; it was based on hate, particularly racial hate; hero worship, the apocalyptic theme of the Third Reich or the Thousand Year Reich; the new golden age for salvation for Germany, exaggerrated nationalism; the easily fostered myth of Aryan racial superiority and the master race. The concept of Lebensraum, room to live, all these ideas were embodied in stereotyped phrases which were constantly repeated. It was all very effective.

Hitler not only exploited every aspect of existing technique in propaganda, in printed media, spectacle, music, symbolism, but also he was the first to make intensive use of two new ones, radio and cinema. He also contributed a ruthless exploitation of emotive mistruth and violence. In total, therefore, he probably wielded the most successful and surprisingly effective propaganda machine ever known. It persuaded a reasonably mature nation (admittedly one deeply shocked by recent defeat in war and current economic disaster), to accept one of the most unpleasant governments ever known in history and to connive at a prolonged aggressive war and genocide. The effects were not deep enough to withstand failure and defeat, but the moral enslavement of so many millions for twelve years remains a remarkable achievement of media exploitation.

Hitler's realisation of the importance of propaganda was crucial. As he put it, 'without the motor car, sound films and wireless there would be no victory for the National Socialist Party'. He believed that a people would be 'filled with a stronger sense of mental security by teaching that brooks no rival than by one which offers a liberal choice', and 'Why demoralise the enemy by arms if you can do so more cheaply by other measures, creating panic, indecision and mental confusion by propaganda. Above all, he realised the effectiveness of short, sharp concentrated campaigns, devoted to a single objective.

Hitler's two greatest assistants in this sphere were Goebbels and Speer. Goebbels, a brilliant speaker in the emotive demagogic tradition like Hitler, and an experienced publicist after his period with Strasser, gave a remarkable lecture on propaganda at Weimar. He analysed the relative effectiveness of press, poster and speeches, but added that in radio, 'We have a great potential for influencing public opinion. I prophesy the day when every factory, every cinema, theatre, market place and store, railway station and every home will be within range of the Fuhrer's voice'. Hitler agreed and already the anti-Nazi parties were beginning to grumble about the subliminal power of radio. The other assistant, Speer, was by training an architect and played for Hitler the role which the painter David had played for Robespierre. He treated the rally or public spectacle as an artistic propaganda medium which required as much detailed design planning as a massive theatrical production.

Together Goebbels and Speer made a considerable contribution to Hitler's propaganda effort, as did some lesser assistants such as the press chief Otto Dietrich, but the overall concept was undoubtedly Hitler's own. In so far as he did consciously imitate, he certainly had been impressed by Northcliffe's organisation of British war propaganda in the last year or so of the Great War, largely because German Imperial propaganda had by that time become very stilted and unadaptable in the Prussian mould, and was therefore much less successful. The other sources of inspiration were Italy where the ritual side of Fascism had really been evolved by the poet D'Annunzio, the short lived dictator of Fiume, Mussolini to a lesser extent, and closer to home, by Luegar, the extrovert Mayor of Vienna.

In terms of Hitler's first propaganda attempts we can trace a steady development from small beginnings with limited funds. In 1920 when his main objective was to get party membership above double figures, he was using duplicated sheets to publicise their meetings; when he was able to afford small advertisement in the Munich *Beobachter;* soon he had such papers in his pocket and ultimately total media control. In terms of technique his main themes are evident right from the start; the use of simple, brutal words like hate, bash, kill; simple repetitive concepts and constant unabashed attack.

There were six main Nazi media of communication. The first of these, not in order of priority so much as seniority, was the press.

One of the weaknesses of the Weimar Republic was its splintered press. They were too many small papers with provincial or party loyalties, no strong nationals able to stand up against Hitler. One important newspaper owner, Hugenburg, a fanatical German nationalist, who had interests also in news agencies and the film industry, gave Hitler massive publicity in the late twenties and co-operated in an anti-reparation campaign. It was Hugenburg and Otto Dietrich, who had married into the *Rheinisch-Westfalische Zeitung,* who introduced Hitler to the Ruhr industrialists. They now began to subsidise him and in effect pay for his propaganda campaigns. Another significant helper in the early press propaganda was Dietrich Eckart, a Bavarian literary man who helped buy and then edited the *Volkischer Beobachter* (Racist Observer), which in 1920 became the party's own weekly paper. While, as Bullock puts it, 'Hitler showed a marked preference for the spoken word over the written word', the help he had from press publicity from Hugenburg and Eckart, and the Thyssen Reichsmarks which came in its wake was vitally important in turning him into a national figure. He exploited his trial in 1923 (the same year that the *Volkische Beobachter,* was increased from weekly to daily publication), as a quasi-martyrdom situation. Thereafter, it was to be printed simultaneously in three cities and ultimately achieved a readership equivalent to 52% of the German people.

The characteristics of the Nazi press were boldness, simplicity and aggression, very different from the dull doctrinal Russian papers of Lenin and Stalin. Goebbels, whose special pride was *Das Reich,* a prestige paper with a circulation around a million, said, 'the reader should get the impression that the writer is in fact a speaker standing beside him, an aura of sweat, leather and blood lust'. Similarly, *Der Sturmer* founded by Julius Streicher was the vehicle for crude anti-semitism. It had a circulation of over half a million and produced such classic headlines as, 'The Jew Rosenfelder sees reason and hangs himself', and with reference to the Weimar government the charming 'World champion belly crawlers'. It also did the classic conspiracy trick with the clever forgery of the 'Protocols of Zion'.

Total circulation of newspapers rose slowly during the Nazi period, from 20 million in 1934 to 26 million in 1943, but it is significant that in the same period sales of escapist pulp magazines doubled from ten to twenty million.

Radio undoubtedly was a Nazi success story. It was used extensively and intensively as a propaganda medium for the first time. This was assisted by a number of technical manoeuvres. The first was the production of the new cheap VE sets (Volksempfanger), which could only take one channel. Over three million of them were sold. Overall listening rose from 4½ to 16 million between 1933 and 1942, helped by the second manoeuvre which was the compulsory installation of radios with loudspeakers in cafés and most public places. The third trick was the use of Radio Wardens to check up that people were listening to the right station. The combination of an almost weekly broadcast by Hitler himself, as happened in 1933, and an emotive diet of specially chosen music and cybernetic news was very powerful. Strauss military marches were important, with Beethoven's *Eroica* on Hitler's birthday; also popular folk music, but not too hot; no saxophones, as they were decadent; Forces favourites on Sunday as the most popular programme; Lili Marlene, Wagner and Horst Wessel became part of Germany's audible environment; the image of the Third Reich in sound. Fanfares in factories, marches for soldiers, it was all part of the Nazi muzak.

Specifically, radio had a number of successes, perhaps the greatest, its contribution to winning the Saar plebiscite in 1936. Goebbels cunningly subsidised the sale of large numbers of VE sets in the Saar prior to the promised secret ballot organised by the League of Nations. The anti-Nazi leader of the Saar, Max Brawn was smeared as being anti-German, and the immediacy of radio was exploited to announce at the last minute that Brawn had fled the Saar the day before the plebiscite. It was too late and too difficult to counteract such a lie with other media, so that even when Brawn drove through the streets he was called an imposter. Radio also had the capacity to cross frontiers — the use of Haw-Haw to broadcast to the British was one rather ineffectual example. Ferdonnet, the French traitor broadcasting from Stuttgart was much more effective. The French soldiers on the Maginot Line with their microsoldat receivers were a vulnerable prey. Radio made the conquest of France much easier.

In the Nazi cinema, the technical standard was again high, with directors of great creative ability such as Leni Riefenstahl who filmed the Olympic Games and the Nuremberg rallies. The image building power of film was appreciated, German history and mythology quarried for allegorical material. There was Riefenstahl's use of the Odin myth in Nuremburg for the *Triumph of Will,* and a biography of Frederick the Great was a vehicle for boosting Hitler as a great German hero. *Ohn Kruger,* a film about the Boer War gave plenty of opportunity for knocking the British. But, in general, the tendency of German war and love films, the basic cinema diet, was to project an image of male comradeship in battle, with racially superior Germans, inferior Jews and others, and a little sadism. The great box office success of the Nazi period was a purely escapist story of a soldier's love, *Grosse Liebe* which was seen by 28 million people. It glorified death in battle, though only enemy casualties were shown on the screen. Goebbels, we are told,

was a great admirer of Eisenstein's *Potemkin* and when briefing
the director for his new *Victory in the West* suggested that he
should imitate the style; odd angles to heighten emotional
involvement, powerful music synchronised with the action to
emphasise dramatic points and foreshortening of figures to obtain
the heroic quality of historical giants. Indeed film, as a form
of intimidation, could be very effective. The showing in Norway
of the invasion of Poland had a considerable effect in demoralising the Norwegians in 1939.

Nazi use of the poster was also significant. Red was almost
the standard colour in the early days, used as Bullock claims,
to provoke the Left. The posters mostly had large, crude illustrations or heavy dominating slogans. The anti-semitic posters
combining swastika and star of David hardly needed words.
The massive 'Ja' posters used in Austria before the plebiscite
on Anschluss, combined with dominating exposure of Hitler's
portrait and hard dramatic slogans like '*Schluss mit der
Korruption*' or '*Sieg um jeden preis*' and '*Ein Kampf, ein Sieg*',
the massive repetition of swastika displays provided a total
outdoor advertising campaign which, when combined with
the press and radio, must have been almost overwhelming.
Hitler's winter relief campaigns, war charity effeorts, made
extensive use of poster displays. The Hitler as a knight in
shining armour approach, was reminiscent of the same theme
used by the Kaiser. In terms of poster artistry he had such
fine practitioners as Hohlwein. Both quantity and quality,
therefore, were considerable.

Fifthly, another of the Nazi media, *par excellence,* was
spectacle. Speer turned mass rallies almost into an art form.
The drill patterns of the old imperial army provided a starting
point and rallies were a feature of Nazi ritual from a very early
stage. The setting chosen was spectacular in itself; Nuremberg
provided a scenic backdrop full of appropriate historical
reminders, and the effect of lighting up the old castle at night
was spectacular. The organisation required was considerable;
huge camps for the participants, split-second timing, with Hitler's
arrival timed for the climax. Then large masses of human beings
were arranged in patterns, with swastikas, eagles and torches.
The lighting was dramatic. Sir Neville Henderson described the
effect aptly as 'a cathedral of ice'. A neon-lit eagle of massive
proportions formed a focal point. The sound effects too were

controlled, with martial music of proven emotive power. The 1938 Nuremberg rally lasted eight days and its cost was enormous. But as the rhythmic, *Sieg Heils* built up to the personal appearance of Goebbels and Hitler, with their carefully studied ability to bring the crowd to hysteria, the total effect must have been so great that dissent was unimaginable. As Huxley put it, 'if exposed long enough to tom-toms and the singing, every one of our philosophers would end by capering and howling like savages'. This was the 'downward transcendence by means of herd intoxication'. With Hitler's funds and his media control it was almost too easy for him, and hardly surprising that he should despise the 'great stupid flock', which appeared just like propaganda fodder to him. What perhaps he failed to appreciate was that his flock must come to realise that they were being controlled. Apart from Speer's new tricks, better amplifiers, brighter lights, there was nothing very different between the Nuremberg rallies and the rallies of Rome, or the Middle Ages or the French Revolution. As Churchill is supposed to have said of Eden on one occasion, 'he combined every cliché in the repertoire except 'God is love' and 'please adjust your dress before leaving. ''.

There were of course many other rituals contributing to this aspect of Nazi cybernetics; the initiation of Hitler Youth, medals for heroes, wreaths for martyrs, the black crêpe banners of Hindenberg's awesome funeral, the ritual of the goose-step which itself sounded like a rhythmic menacing form of audio-intimidation.

Hitler's ancillary media included a multiplicity of little visual symbols, by which the Reich co-ordinated its image. Above all, there was the swastika or Hakenkreuz adopted by the Austrian German National Socialist Workers' Party in 1918, cleverly put on a red background by Hitler and presented in massive quantities in a co-ordinated visual corporate identity programme of great efficiency. The use of uniforms to depersonalise and militarise was also clever. Brown shirts; the Italians had black, Garibaldi before them had used red for much the same purpose. Jackboots, flags, eagles, the skull and crossbones badge for the Gestapo, all contributed to the visual projection of Nazism. Sculpture, too, played a predictable role, with Aryan heroes featuring, Horst Wessel among them, and Hitler himself in a typical heroic pose. Architecture was becoming an obsession with Hitler, particularly massive triumphal arches, stadia and imperial type palaces of classical style. However, little was actually built.

In the deployment of media by Hitler and his assistants, it can be seen that in combination their penetration, repetition, frequency and power were considerable. Control was absolute and no aspect of life was untouched. Even the education of the young, as in Soviet Russia was geared to the Hitler Youth, founded by the anti-semitic teacher Streicher, with its ritual ladder of promotion, and regimented adulation of Nazi virtues. Given the media control and the style or technique which we have also touched on, we come lastly to the choice of theme and message content. Certainly, he adhered to his principles of projecting a few simple ideas and avoiding the abstract themes. His language and that of the other Nazis, both written and spoken, was very straight-forward. Crude, and using short violent words, it was aimed at the lowest intellect; in all a deliberately provocative style full of aggression and cutting innuendo. Issues were over-simplified and reality ignored. Reliance was placed on shattering criticism expressed in emotive language. It was hard to contradict. The Versailles traitors, the November criminals who had betrayed Germany at the end of the First World War, the Jews and Communists who could be condemned in similar hooligan terms. Use was made of simple metaphors like comparing Jews with rats, but nothing more complicated. There were also a number of good mnemonics 'Deutschland Erwache' 'The Thousand Year Reich', emotive words like, 'Einkreisung' encirclement, 'Herrenvolk (the Master race) and 'Lebensraum' (usally translated 'a place in the sun'), but they all embodied happy promises of revenge, revival and success. They appealed to vanity, insecurity or ambition. Not only were these rhythmic incantations of palatable clichés delivered at high emotional pitch but looming over all was the constant threat of violence. The concentration camps were not kept secret but used as propaganda like the S.S. and other symbols of intimidation.

For all its crudity Hitler's propaganda did sometimes achieve heights of subtlety. For example, the use of the railway coach at Compiegne (previously used for the German surrender in 1918) for France's surrender to Hitler was a clever touch. The total projection from 1920 when Hitler took over propaganda for the party until 1941 when the image began to crack, was masterly. It was undoubtedly made easier for him than it would have been in another period or country by the German people's double shock of military and economic humiliation, the availability of vulnerable scapegoats and popular themes which could be exploited. He was also helped by getting so much industrial money to buy newspapers, the *Beobachter,* initially, with more later.

While Mussolini is generally recognised as having been a very competent propagandist in the same mould as Hitler, the achievement of the Spanish Falange and its Blue Shirts has perhaps been under-rated. Its performance in South America with a rapid conversion of over one million people was in many ways very remarkable. Brazil had its Green Shirts, Mexico its Golden Shirts. Fascism had the multi-media appeal to work from North Africa to the Argentine.

MODERN CHINA

China, which had a rich tradition of contribution to media development (it invented paper and printing) also provides an example of highly imaginative modern propaganda overcoming huge difficulties of space, language and ignorance. With a huge population and low rate of literacy, penetration of mass media was still low during the succession of political upheavals which coincided with the career of Mao Tse Tung. Given perhaps a degree of naïve credulity in the Chinese people in political matters the propaganda of the Chinese communists shows an imaginative, poetic quality which is remarkable.

Mao and many of his assistants had the benefit of some Russian training in propaganda arts, but Mao in particular contributed a special panache, sense of imagery and feeling for the cybernetic needs of a large population which was quite un-Russian. His personal cultivation of heroic stature with the Great March of 1934 gave a gigantic mythical quality. The crossing of the Liutung Bridge over the Taku River in 1935 painted in heroic style by Li Tsing Tsin is a prototype of the genre. More recently the swim down the Yangtse gave his whole conduct a touch of Confucius and a medieval warlord. In his own words, 'Our people are poor and blank, but the most beautiful poem can be written on a blank sheet of paper'.

Audience understanding was a key part of the Chinese communist propaganda. As early as 1925 they were saying, 'In our propaganda we must know and examine the opinion of the masses, which is necessary in guiding them'. From this came the development of 'mass line' conversion campaigns, accompanied by intensive recruitment to the Red Guard. Propaganda was less doctrinaire, brighter and given such frills as the Yangko dance.

The propaganda development of Mao had its beginnings early in his career. He had a stroke of luck in media terms in that in 1938 the *New China Daily,* the Communists' main organ was allowed to be published by the Chiang Kai Chek government simply because the Communists were contributing to the anti-Japanese war effort, and had some international sympathy. The basis of a Marxist propaganda infrastructure had been built up since 1920 and the resistance atmosphere of the late Thirties helped it. The relative success of the Communists as opposed to the Kuomintang against the Japanese made their succession to power after the war almost a matter of course, but throughout the period there were some gifted propagandists working for Mao. Teng To for instance the poet and satirist was editor of the *Peking Peoples' Daily,* organ of the Central Committee and supported Mao strongly from 1938-1949, though he later attacked Mao's policy of foreign aggression. The early post-war propaganda period was straightforward. In 1949 Lo Jui Ching launched 'the campaign for suppression of anti-revolutionaries with fanfare' aimed mainly at the traditional corruption of Chinese bureaucracy. There were five targets; bribery, tax evasion, cheating, theft and spying. Because of low literacy, in 1953 Li Chin commented that 'conversation is the best form of propaganda', the encouragement of reading groups was important. In Shantung in 1952 there were 450,000 propagandist newspaper reading groups, which together with the wall newspapers greatly increased effective penetration.

More imaginative campaigns followed — The Hundred Flowers campaign of 1957, 'Let a hundred flowers blossom, a hundred schools of thought'. Then in the following year came the 'Great Leap Forward', to project the new economic expansion and technological revolution. In this period, Peng Chen controlled propaganda for Mao with the help of Chow

Yung, editor of the *Literary Gazette*. He organised the output of popular parables based on the theme of good peasants against bad land-lords. One theme was, 'Support for the three Red Banners; party line, Great People's Communes and the Great Leap Forward'. As Mao put it at this time, 'art is neither more nor less than a major weapon in the revolutionary class struggle', and from 1949 'The Chinese people, one quarter of the human race, have now stood up'. Another important change of this period was the replacement of classical Chinese by the vernacular in a new simplified alphabet. Writers like Lu Hsun who wrote the propagandist tale 'The True Story of Ah Q' supported this move. The typical fable of the new era was short and simple. For example:

Once soldiers of a people's Liberation Army unit's First Company went to the Red Star production team for field training. The weather was very dry, so they helped the commune members fight the drought. One day the company commander borrowed two water jars from the house of Aunt Zhang, a poor peasant. One of them was broken during the work due to carelessness by the leader of the Sixth Squad. That evening he brought a new jar and returned it to Aunt Zhang. The first time he sent it to her, she asked her grandson to take it back. It was dispatched to her a second time. Before long someone called out at the door.

When the Sixth Squad leader opened the door, there was the child who put down the jar at the entrance. He smiled and said, "Grandma asked me to bring it back again."

"Listen, little friend, take it back to your Grandma and say that damaged things must be replaced."

"No, Grandma said there is no need to replace the broken jar because the PLA uncles are helping our production team fight the drought." With these words, he ran away.

The Sixth Squad leader took the jar to Aunt's house for a third time and explained to her over and over that Chairman Mao teaches that damaged things must be replaced. Revolutionary discipline is one of the glorious traditions of the People's Liberation Army.

When she heard this Aunt Zhang was deeply moved.

"Fine, I'll take it, I'll keep it and often tell its story so that everyone can learn from the PLA to be models of discipline."

In spite of the success of this period there was considerable disillusionment in the 'Great Leap Forward', and as Mao's career appeared to be waning, rival groups began to fight for cybernetic control. In the 1959-1966 period three main papers on the Maoist side, the *Red Flag, People's Daily* and *Liberation Army,* vied with those controlled by the Peking committee, the *Peking Daily, Peking Evening News* and *Front Line.* From this stalemate, Mao produced his propagandist *tour de force,* the Cultural Revolution, with himself playing the leading role. He began with spectacular stunts; his famous Yangtse swim of nine miles in 65 minutes at the age of 73, a string of good will tours and a re-enactment of the heroic march of 1934. *The East is Red* and the new hit song for the occasion *Sailing the Seas we depend on the Helmsman,* plus *Battle Song of the Red Guards.* Red plastic copies of the Chairman's thoughts were issued in vast numbers. Massive crowds gathered to chant 'Mao Tse Tung' in unison, and 'Mao is the red, red sun in our hearts'. Huge red banners and portraits dominated the scene and Mao's men exploited crowd emotion as totally as Hitler had done, creating ecstatic, hysterical mobs with rhythmic chanting, crying and violence.

Amongst Mao's assistants, at this stage, was his fourth wife Chiang Ching, a former actress who encouraged opera and theatre as propaganda media. Films and plays about corrupt mandarins formed the background for discrediting a number of Mao's enemies. They were reverting to capitalism; he was the symbolic hero of the revolution. The massive posters of the cultural revolution showed always Mao in heroic pose, paternal and benevolent and slogans such as, 'Proletarian Revolutionaries rise up and unite under the great red flag of Chairman Mao's thoughts'. At the same time, the new culture involved destroying the old, and since 'The Revolution touches the soul of everyman' it required symbolic acts of violence and vandalism; the burning of the art galleries, and the humiliation of university professors. The régime was based on a red mythology of long marches, long swims and mystical sayings; its justification was emotional rather than intellectual. Certain people had to be hated; bankers,

Americans and intellectuals. Mao had to be loved. There were orgies of group confession before excited crowds, children denouncing parents, a subjection of individuality to the little red book and its author. Once the political objective of unified Maoist rule had been achieved, together now with monopoly of media control, it was time to end the violence and dispense with those who had inflicted it on his behalf.

The Red Guard, itself a temporary cellular medium, had to go. The very hysterical nature of its original role meant that it could never be steady and reliable. Instead, in 1968, Mao set up the Worker's Propaganda Team to take over from the Red Guard as the corporate heroes of China, owing total obedience to Mao. The party workers were to be trained as 'a transmission belt between party and population', reading aloud Mao's papers to the illiterate in the villages.

Given that China's literacy rate in 1949 was around 15% the achievement of Communism in general and Mao in particular, in obtaining such effective penetration of ideas is considerable.

In media terms, the special characteristics have been the adaptation of mass media, both printed and electronic, to the difficult target of a massive population living at subsistence level and largely uneducated; a two stage use of media with field propagandists. In style terms we have seen that poster and graphic presentation has been more western than oriental, just as China's new cybernetic music has a strong western or at least Russian flavour. The message treatment has tended to be straightforward; simple metaphors like 'the hundred flowers', the constant use of red, the colour and the word, in the red book, red flag, red sun, red thoughts and so on. Also the propaganda has been laced with love and hate figures; easily understandable extremes; bankers, Americans and intellectuals to be hated; Mao to be idolised. Violence also has been important; denunciation and humiliation of deviants, brainwashing of those who resist, using the total Pavlov technique; isolation, intimidation, abuse, disorientation and physical deprivation to leave the majority of those subjected to it in a state of nervous breakdown. But, in terms of such a massive population, the numbers are probably minute. The mass spectacles, tens of thousands of identical gymnasts making huge human symbols, typify not just the ability to project images but to use the target audience to create the symbols, reinforcement by participation. This type of spectacle, was copied from the Russians and is now taught by the Chinese to the emergent African states, which form an important arena for Maoist propaganda.

DEMOCRACY AND THE WESTERN WORLD

Since the last three examples have all been from totalitarian states with media monopoly, it may be useful to review, if only briefly, the significance of modern propaganda usage in Western Europe and the United States. Clearly, there has been a considerable advance in the technological skills of the media and the sophistication both of the communicators and the audiences. In particular, the application of commercial expertise from research and advertising to the projection of political and religious messages has drawn considerable criticism. Vance Packard's worried critique of the symbol manipulators, who invaded American politics in the 1950's is legendary. The 1952 'I like Ike' campaign, for Eisenhower's presidential candidature, managed by the advertising agency BBDO; the creation of Kennedy as a war hero; the grooming of Richard Nixon by Murray Chotiner; the remark of Rosser Reeves, another advertising man who helped Eisenhower in the 1956 elections that the two political parties were 'just like two competing brands of toothpaste'; the stage management of the 1956 Republican convention by MGM and an $8 million dollar campaign for the democrats by Norman Craig and Kummel, (more famous for the Maidenform bra dream); all these events were seen as the downward path, not just into commercialisation of politics, but a new seduction technique for the masses. Clearly such techniques do quite frequently put a gloss on political performance which makes politicians or parties look better than they really are. The huge expenditure of advertising money which made possible Nixon's come back in 1968, and the strains on morality of having to collect advertising money in 1972 show the problem. But, as we have seen in nearly every period, communicators of both political and religious ideas have used whatever techniques were available. Symbols have been manipulated since the days of the Pharoahs. In terms of cybernetic skill the difference between Caesar or Urban II and

Hitler or John F. Kennedy is one of detail rather than principle. Where a really major difference does lie, is between States where there is a media monopoly, such as Nazi Germany, Napoleonic France or Soviet Russia, where the populations are fed with ideas from one source only, and non-totalitarian States where there is, at least, some sort of choice. The quality of image projection in non-totalitarian States may, at times, be higher than in totalitarian ones, simply because each party or sect has to compete with others. There are certain attractions, perhaps, about the way in which the Communists in both Russia and China manage to project a coherent cybernetic image which covers almost every aspect of life. It is neat and tidy, and must, as Hitler said of the no-choice situation, lead to some mental security. The western system is much untidier. It allows for a massive communications input from commercial advertisers, who may exploit all kinds of weaknesses to increase their sales. In so doing it can create attitudes which are materialistic, anti-social, unhealthy or otherwise undesirable. At the same time, the masses are given no clear cybernetic guidance. Except in wartime or other national disasters there is little attempt even to foster nationalism. There is no coherent projection of a total concept of life, simply because this is left to individual parties or sects or institutions who may have the money or vitality to project their ideals through the mass media. They have the problems of access and competition. The populations are exposed to a multiplicity of often conflicting ideas, projected with entirely different and often suspect motivations. Any evaluation of such a situation must depend on whether the individual believes that in the end good attitudes will be projected best and listened to most, or whether he prefers the totalitarian exclusion of choice and the entrustment of attitude forming to those in power.

British propaganda in the twentieth century has often been brilliant in the two periods of war, fairly complacent and dull for the rest. 'Let's go with Labour', 'Action not words' from the Tories, 'Yesterday's men' from Labour, 'Life's better with the Tories', 'You've never had it so good' British party propaganda remains inhibited and unexciting. All the main parties use advertising agencies, but failed to project a consistent image and lack the will or the money to co-ordinate all available media. The double piece of governmental propaganda, 'Yes —

for the Common Market' and 'No — for the Common Market', organised in 1975, with one government financing a campaign for both sides, totally lacked cybernetic confidence and was utterly uninspiring. Nevertheless, perhaps it treated the population as democratically mature rather than as propaganda fodder. The Labour party's schizophrenia over cybernetics was seen in the 1975 counter - inflation propaganda campaign. It realised that there was a major attitude changing task to be done, and that propaganda was a method of preventing runaway inflation, but refused to let the Central Office of Information handle the campaign, because its recent fuel saving campaign had, though successful, been too glossily professional.

Self-consciousness about the use of the media for other directedness was shown at its height by Riesman's famous analysis of *Toodle the Engine,* as a training of children for conformity. The use by artists, advertisers, politicians and priests of propaganda tricks for the engineering of consent excited worries. Role playing, status, celebrities, fashion, greed; whatever reaction is exploited, it is inevitable in a free society that most of these age-old tricks will be adapted to new media and new needs. The clenched fist of black power or the raised rifle of El Fatah, the torch of women's liberation are all part of the mixture. What the democratic governments may envy the totalitarian ones, is their greater ability to project a self-denial ethic, to control confidence and to lead without too many questions.

The classic symbol of the weakness of underground media in the modern totalitarian state, is the picture of hand printed posters (fly posting is one of the few media that a resistance can use easily), being torn down by the invading Russian soldiers in the attack on Czechoslovakia in 1968. The mobilisation of public opinion in such a situation was difficult. It becomes a question of who has the tanks to hold the radio station.

In terms of religious propaganda a number of sects have shown a capacity to adapt to the media requirements of the twentieth century. The Pentecostal Church, a Holy Roller type of approach using simple tongue language, has flourished, particularly in Scandinavia, Brazil and Nigeria. In 1918 Mrs McPherson of Los Angeles built a temple and drove a motor bike onto the stage shouting, 'Stop, you're going to hell'. The strong simple appeal to people who have for one reason or another becomes rootless. The Seventh Day Adventists, use the old millennial theme which we have seen used also in Rome, the Middle Ages and by Hitler. It flourished in hard times, but always had a problem when the promised Day of Judgement arrived and nothing happened. Jehovah's Witnesses, another powerful sect, started in 1874 by Charles Russell in Pittsburg, also preached the millennial theme, and had a skilful propaganda network based on print; Zion's *Watchtower* Tract and door-to-door canvassing. One of its slogans, 'Millions now living will never die', summed up the quality of its message and amongst other areas it had great success in Zambia. The quality of message penetration was proved by the special resistance to Gestapo torture put up by members of this sect. Another sect, with a basis of print and publishing was Christian Science, founded by Mary Baker Eddy in 1869, with the slogan 'God is Mind'; the main medium the *Christian Science Monitor,* and the main target audience middle class middle-aged females. A variant on Christian Science produced by Frank Robinson of Idaho was the first religion to be marketed by mail order advertising as a correspondence course — he sold a million of them by 1930 on the theme 'I talked with God'.

Particularly interesting from a propaganda point of view amongst the modern Christian sects was the Salvation Army since it exploited so many techniques. Founded by Booth, a Methodist, in 1878 it used army drill, uniform and music as a sort of extended metaphor, had its symbol — an S, its newspapers, including *The War Cry,* with circulation estimated at around two million; its moto 'Blood and Fire'; its crimson flag and its rituals of public confessions, witnessing and emotive preaching. Its main message, 'Joy', was simple and effective and Booth himself a very able publicist, who used metaphor, trick effects, said he would beat a drum standing on his head if it meant an extra convert. Apart from its considerable success in the western world, its simple appeal and fairly primitive rituals also achieved remarkable results in underdeveloped areas such as the Congo, where its drive against witch doctors was fortuitously helped by a confusion of the S with a popular Baptist martyr whose name began with that letter.

The Mormons, the Radio Church of God, the snake handling churches of Tennessee, provide other examples of modern media usage by Christian sects. Moral Rearmament was based on print,

I

pyramid and theatres. On the non-Christian front Soka Gakkai was a Japanese sect using a disciplined hierarchy to project a Quaker type message. Also Rama Krishna was typical of newer meditational type cults appealing internationally to a young age group.

The only generalisation one might make about cult media projection in the last hundred years is that, perhaps, it is easier for extremist ideas, with novelty to the point almost of freakishness to attract attention on the crowded wavelengths of the world free media, than for the totally straighforward.

In the late 20th century there are four over-riding features in the propaganda structure of the free world.

The first is communication overload. This is attributable to the fact that any institution which has the power, money or skill can gain access to the mass media; so there is an enormous clutter of conflicting attempted manipulations of the individual.

Secondly, cybernetics in most countries and the free world as a whole lack any central direction. What could be regarded as major requirements of attitude change or development are neglected or left to agencies with outdated styles and inadequate resources. The established churches, for instance, in most western countries once had a crucial role in moral cybernetics; this they can no longer perform, but no alternative agencies have taken it over. Apart from the enforcement of law and order most media organisations have no great stake in any broad promotion of ethics. Even the various educational systems are by and large not committed to more than a small portion of this role.

Thirdly, much greater resources are devoted quite frequently to cybernetic objectives which are by any standards trivial; commercial branding, sports and entertainment promotions, artificial political issues.

Fourthly, given the lack of any strong and consistent cybernetic leads, populations are vulnerable to quite sudden, unexpected and irrational penetration by new concepts which may be trivial or damaging in their objectives and freakish in their presentation. Even though, audience sophistication improves with increased exposure to different media, and the power of propaganda is often realised, semi - voluntary susceptibility remains.

The case for improved analysis of propaganda objectives and techniques is therefore considerable, as is the case for general education on media usage. Above all, the goals of society should be discussed and defined in relation to media practice. The whole concept of democracy and majority decisions can be reduced to absurdity if there is realisation that majority attitudes are largely the product of previous cybernetics. The period 1935-55 was as a whole a period in most parts of the free world of fairly strong cybernetics. Since then, many of the traditional cybernetic themes: willingness to fight for home and country, the family system, freedom, progress, have lost credibility, and the media are more reluctant to state a point of view.

*   *   *   *

The development of propaganda in and to the so-called Third World presents some interesting examples of technique. In general terms, communication from developed to underdeveloped countries is often poor, largely because of a failure to adapt message style or content to audiences with different customs or levels of sophistication. The Germans in 1941 were noticeably better in India than the British. The ultimate failure of the Jesuits in the Far East, the partial failure of most European nations in Africa, the strange effects of Christian missionaries in many parts of the world, are all examples. The decolonisation period of Africa shows some of the difficulties. Christian missionaries had often blundered through existing tribal attitudes; the Salvation Army with its drums and uniforms had actually been particularly successful in parts of Africa. Colonial governments like the British, Portugese and French, had been fairly unsubtle in their image projection. Russia and China entered the African scene with the easier propaganda task of projecting a common anti-imperialist image, but they too failed to adapt adequately their style and ideologies to local conditions. The Chinese came closer to it than any perhaps, in that they could claim to be a non-white people who had revolted themselves against European imperialism fifty years before. The Chinese, too, were liberal in providing radio stations and printing equipment to countries like Tanzania. But the emergent African nations have shown a remarkable ability to be eclectic in the propaganda they accept from whatever source.

There are a number of outstanding communicators amongst the leaders of the new African states. Kenyatta, in particular, provides examples of a wide understanding of image cultivation. Born Johnstone Kamau, he acquired the nickname Jomo Kenyatta; Jomo because it sounded more African, Kenyatta the Kikuyu word for the belt of beads which he always wore. Kenyatta showed a remarkable ability to combine the techniques of European propaganda with a deep understanding of tribal motivations. Brought up as a Kikuyu warrior/farmer and educated in the Church of Scotland school he was able to see the distorting effect of one culture superimposing its attitudes on another. 1922 saw the founding of the YKA and an anti-slave labour campaign in the Indian financed *East African Chronicle*. *Muiginthania* followed in 1928 and was the first Kikuyu paper. Kenyatta spent the years 1931-46 in Britain, winning some international sympathy for the Kenyan cause by publishing an authoritative book on his nation's folk lore. He returned to find nationalism growing under the KAO with its black (for the skin), red (for blood), and green (for land) flag. Its frustrations erupted in the violence of Mau Mau, for which Kenyatta was probably unjustly imprisoned. But he used his imprisonment to enhance his role as the natural leader figure of the revolution. His almost divine image as Mzee, his style of hats and fly whisk, his rhythmic calls for *Uhuru* (freedom) and *Harambee* (emotive Swahili exhortation) provided a basis for crowd captivation. His ability to enthuse crowds and the new mythology he built himself enabled him to carry greater weight than many other new African leaders, who rose faster in their careers, but with less solid foundations.

Another example of a Third World leader with a remarkable flair for propaganda was Ghandi, who would have denied the fact hotly. He said, 'Truth embodied in the living example of an individual is far more potent than tons of propaganda based on falsehood . . . . . Truth is self-propagating'. But Ghandi's mastery of metaphor and understanding of his audience was akin to that of any of the great prophets. His policy of non-cooperation was 'A programme of propaganda by reducing profession to practice, not one of compelling others to yield obedience by violence direct or indirect'. 'Satya graha is like a banyan tree with innumerable branches'.

EPILOGUE

Any attempt at an assessment of the proper role of mass persuasion in the modern world is bedevilled with traps. On the one hand, there is the argument that spiritual freedom, protection of the mind from political or moral pollution must be maintained or improved. This leads to demands for reduction of both commercial control on the media in capitalist countries and reduction of political control in totalitarian states. But it is naive to suggest that elimination of one power source in a country from access to its media, means elimination of propaganda, leaving nothing but truth, genuine folk art or culture. It simply allows greater access to different groups of people, who consciously or unconsciously will then try to shape attitudes in their own particular style. The answer to worries about manipulation by any group, commercial or otherwise, is not to censor them, but to make audiences more aware that various groups are trying to manipulate them; how they do it, why and when. The only way to avoid dictatorship of taste, attitude, by one leading group or another is to train audiences to discriminate, particularly by being able to recognise the cruder techniques of emotional cybernetics. Thus a degree of immunisation can be built up. Peoples can be insulated to some extent against the worst effects of propaganda, even of the most subtle kind.

Mass persuasion is happening all the time. While sometimes, it operates in the short term with the quite sudden creation of new attitudes, it will have been seen that human personality does not allow for many deep or lasting changes of attitude within one generation. Far more important are the longer term aspects of mass persuasion; the very much deeper and more long lasting attitudes which are created, perhaps, over two or three generations, permeating all aspects of art and education as well as conventional media, and helping to form basic attitudes on subjects such as war or peace, acquisitiveness or sacrifice, violence or toleration. While recent writers such as J. A. C. Brown rightly show that propaganda has very limited effects, he is referring, by and large, to psychological research conducted in relation to short term campaigns. Brainwashing appears to be even more short term in its effects. But the very deep and underlying prevalence of militarism, imperialism, racism and puritanism in the social media of particular societies, over decades if not centuries is of much greater importance.

The materialist leanings of current Western media over a prolonged period may well be creating an insecurely materialist generation, just as the 19th century media attitude to war created the generations of the early 20th century who started wars. The spreading of these ideas is slow and insidious. It is not necessarily deliberate or controlled by even an identifiable élite, but does quite genuinely trap whole peoples in a lifetime of acquisitiveness or racial hatred or useless conflict or obsessive puritanism. The ideas spread so widely that they become confused with absolute truths. At certain points of history it has been possible or necessary to divert marginally the massive tidal force of such ideas.

It becomes evident that the most dangerous propaganda is the kind which is not recognised as such at all, either by its audience or even by its perpetrators. It is the steady drip, drip of aggressive, prejudiced or materialistic ideas which those competing to be social leaders project through all the media in their fight for personal success. It may involve a change in attitude to the rights of the individual; the importance or otherwise of the State; the importance of life or after-life, of body and soul. It is the massive build-up of overlapping art forms: television, architecture, music, literature, advertising, design, which largely creates the attitudes of the majority and carries a corporate responsibility for so doing, even although it may have fed on the early stages of these same attitudes in order to survive. We have seen the dangers of nationalistic or imperialist art. But there are also great dangers, as Colin Wilson has pointed out, in art which is defeatist.

On the positive side it must be recognised that man thrives on communal motivation. Man's behaviour is governed largely by the complex of attitude forming influences which work on his basic instincts. Planned mass persuasion, with objectives defined, and long term effects thoroughly investigated, must become a more important element in government. With threats to world survival coming from violence, population growth and shortage of raw materials or energy, a logical, non-secretive approach to cybernetics must be taken seriously.

BIBLIOGRAPHY

PART ONE

Aranguren, J. N., *Human Communications,* (transl.), London, 1967.
Bantock, G. H., *Freedom and Authority in Education,* London, 1952.
Barthes, R., *Mythologies* (transl.), London, 1973.
Bartlett, F. C., *Political Propaganda,* Cambridge, 1940.
Bernay, R. M., in Christenson, J., and McWilliam, R. O., ed. *Readings in Public Opinion and Propaganda,* New York, 1971.
Bernays, E. L., *The Engineering of Consent,* New York, 1955.
Black, J. B., *The Coordination and Control of Propaganda,* London, 1969.
Blumler, J., and McQuail, D., *Television in Politics,* London, 1968.
Boorstin, D. J., *The Image,* New York and London, 1962.
Briggs, A., *History of Broadcasting in the United Kingdom,* London, 1961.
Brown, J. A. C., *Techniques of Persuasion,* London, 1963.
Burgelin, O., and Saussure F.de., in McQuail, D., ed. *Sociology of Mass Communications,* London, 1972.
Canetti, E., *Crowds and Power* (transl.), London, 1963.
Carpenter E., and McLuhan, M., *Explorations in Communications,* Boston, 1966.
Carlsmith, J. M., in Rosnow, R. L., and Robinson, E. J., *Experiments in Persuasion,* New York, 1970.
Casey, R. D., *The Press, Propaganda and Pressure Groups,* New York, 1950.
Castles, F. G., *Pressure Groups,* London, 1967.
Carter, D., *The Fourth Branch of Government,* New York, 1959.
Christenson, J., and McWilliam, R. O., ed. *Readings in Public Opinion and Propaganda,* New York, 1971.
Cohn, N., *The Pursuit of the Millennium,* London, 1957.
Cox, D. F., and Bauer, R. A., in Rosnow, *q.v.*
Crossman, R. H. S., *The Politics of Viewing, New Statesman,* Vol. 76, London.
Davison, W. P., *International Communications,* New York, 1968.
Dexter, L. A., and White, D. M., ed. *People, Society and Mass Communications,* London, 1964.
Dickens, A. G., *Luther and the German Nation,* London, 1966.
Domenach, J. M., *La Propagande Politique,* Paris, 1973.
Doob, L. W., *Public Opinion and Propaganda,* London, 1949.
Doob, L. W., *Communication in Africa,* Yale, 1961.
Driencourt, J., *La Propagande, Paris,* 1958.
Ellul, J., *Propaganda: The Formation of Men's Attitudes,* (transl.) New York, 1973.
Enzenburger, H. M., in McQuail, *q.v.*

Fagen, R., *Politics and Communication,* Boston, 1966.
Fesbach, S., in Rosnow, *q.v.*
Festinger, L., and Carlsmith, J. M., in Rosnow, *q.v.*
Fraser, L., *Propaganda,* London, 1957.
Frazer, J. G., *The Golden Bough,* London, 1922.
Freud, S. G., *Group Psychology and the Analysis of the Ego,* New York, 1930.
Gans, H. J., in McQuail, *q.v.*
Gerbner, G., in McQuail, *q.v.*
Gollob, H. F., and Dittes, J. E., in Rosnow, *q.v.*
Grierson, J., *On Documentary,* ed. Forsyth Hardy, London, 1966.
Halloran, J. D., ed. *The Effects of Television,* London, 1966.
Halloran, J. D., Eliot, P., and Murdoch, G., *Demonstrations in Communications,* London, 1972.
Hartman, G. W., in Rosnow, *q.v.*
Hoffer, E., in Christenson, *q.v.*
Hoggart, R., *The Uses of Literacy,* London, 1958.
Hoggart, R., *Speaking to Each Other,* London, 1968.
Hovland, C., and Weiss, W., in Rosnow, *q.v.*
Hovland, C., *Communication and Persuasion,* Yale, 1965.
Huizinga, J., *The Waning of the Middle Ages,* (transl.), London, 1965.
Huntford, R., *The New Totalitarianism,* London, 1972.
Jame, W., *Variety of Religious Experience,* London, 1968.
Johnson, E. D., *Communication,* New York, 1955.
Kahn G., *Europas Fursten in Sittenspiegel der Karikatur,* Stuttgart, 1914.
Katz, D., etc. *Public Opinion and Propaganda,* New York, 1954.
Klapper, J. T., *The Effects of Mass Communication,* New York, 1960.
Knox, R., *Enthusiasm,* Oxford, 1950.
Koestler, A., *Arrow in the Blue,* London, 1958.
Kracauer, S., *The Nature of Film,* New York, 1961.
Lasswell, H. D., and Blumenstock, *World Revolutionary Propaganda,* New York, 1962.
Lasswell, H. D., Carey, R. D., and Smith, B. L., *Propaganda and Promotional Activities,* Chicago, 1969.
Lasswell, H. D., and Kaplan, *Power and Society,* New York, 1949.
Lasswell, H. D., *Propaganda Techniques in the First World War,* New York, 1927.
Lazarsfield, P. F., and Merton, R. K., *Mass Communication, Popular Taste and Organised Social Action,* New York, 1969.
Lippmann, W., *Public Opinion,* New York, 1922.
McLuhan, M., *Understanding Media,* London, 1964.
McQuail, D., *Towards a Sociology of Mass Communications,* London, 1969.
McQuail, D., ed. *Sociology of Mass Communications,* London, 1972.
Maguire, W. J., in Rosnow, *q.v.*
Merton, R. K., in McQuail, *q.v.*
Metzl, E., *The Poster,* London, 1963.
Miller, G., *The Psychology of Communications,* London, 1970.
Mitchell, M. G., *Propaganda Polls and Public Opinion,* New York, 1970.
Noelle-Neumann, E., in Rosnow, *q.v.*
Nordenstreng, K., in McQuail, *q.v.*
Packard, V., *The Hidden Persuaders,* New York, 1957.

Plato, *The Republic*, (transl.), London, 1960.
Pye, L., *Communications and Political Development*, New York, 1963.
Quatter, T. H., *Propaganda and Psychological Warfare*, London, 1952.
Raglan, Lord., *The Hero: A Study in Tradition, Myth and Drama*,
    London, 1936.
Rhode, E., *A History of the Cinema*, London, 1966.
Rickards, M., *Posters of Protest and Revolution*, Bath, 1970.
Rose, R., *Influencing Voters*, London, 1967.
Rosnow, R. L., and Robinson, E. J., *Experiments in Persuasion*, New
    York, 1969.
Sargant, W., *The Battle for the Mind*, London, 1957.
Schramm, W., *Responsibility in Mass Communications*, Chicago, 1969.
Schramm, W., ed. *Mass Communications*, Chicago, 1960.
Schramm, W., *The Process and Effects of Mass Communication*, Chicago,
    1971.
Schramm, W., *Mass Media and National Development*, Stanford, 1963.
Siepmann, L. A., in Christenson, *q.v.*
Smith, B. L., and C. M., *International Communications and Public Opinion*,
    Princeton, 1956.
Smith, B. L., and Casey, R. D., *Propaganda, Communications and Public
    Opinion*, Princeton, 1946.
Smythe, D. W., in McQuail, *q.v.*
Sorokin, P. A., in Rosnow, *q.v.*
Suedfield, P., and Vernon, J., in Rosnow, *q.v.*
Trenaman, J., *Television and Political Image*, London, 1959.
Tunstall, J., ed. *Media Sociology*, London, 1970.
Ullmann, W., *Principles of Government and Politics in the Middle Ages*,
    Cambridge, 1961.
Vernon, M. D., *Human Motivation*, London, 1968.
Westrup, J., *Introduction to Musical History*, London, 1957.
Williams, R., *Communications*, London, 1962.
Wilson, C. H., *Parliament, People and Mass Media*, London, 1962.
Windelsham, Lord, *Communications and Political Power*, London, 1974.
Wright, C. R., *Mass Communications*, London, 1959.
Zimbardo, P. G., in Rosnow, *q.v.*

PART TWO

Adelman, P., *Gladstone and Disraeli in Victorian Politics*, London, 1970.
Allen, W. S., *The Nazi Seizure of Power*, London, 1966.
Atherton, J. M., *Political Prints in the Age of Hogarth*, London, 1965.
Balfour, M., *The Kaiser and his Times*, London, 1964.
Barclay, W., *Communicating the Gospel*, London, 1962.
Belder, E. A., *Propaganda in the Thirty Years War*, Princeton, 1940.   z
Berger, C., *Broadsides and Bayonets*, Philadelphia, 1961.
Berlin, I., *Karl Marx*, London, 1948.
Bransted, E. K., *Goebbels and National Socialist Propaganda*, London, 1968.
Briggs, A., *History of Broadcasting in the United Kingdom*, Vol. III,
    London, 1975.
Briggs, A., *Public Opinion and Public Health in the Age of Chadwick*,
    London, 1948.

Bullock, A., *Hitler: A Study in Tyranny*, London, 1952.
Burckhardt, J., *The Civilization of the Renaissance in Italy*, (transl.), London, 1898.
Calder, A., *The People's War: 1939-1945*, London, 1970.
Carr, E. H., *The Bolshevik Revolution, London*, 1950-1964.
Carr, E. H., *What is History?*, London, 1964.
Child, H., and Cobles, D., *Christian Symbols*, London, 1960.
Cobban, R., *History of France*, London, 1957.
Cobban, R., *Aspects of the French Revolution*, London, 1971.
Cohn, N., *The Pursuit of the Millennium*, London, 1957.
Cohn, N., *Warrant for Genocide*, London, 1960.
Collier, R., *The General Next to God: William Booth*, London, 1956.
Cooke, A., *America*, London, 1966.
Elegant, R. S., *Mao's Great Revolution*, London, 1970.
Fraser, A., *Cromwell*, London, 1974.
Freeman, G., *The Schoolgirl Ethic: The Life and Work of Angela Brazil*, London, 1976.
George, M. D., *The Political Caricature*, London, 1961.
Grant, M., *Roman Coins: From Imperium to Auctoritas*, London, 1946.
Green, M., *Evangelism and the Early Church*, London, 1964.
Grunberger, R., *Social History of the Third Reich*, London, 1964.
Hitler, A., *Mein Kampf*, (transl.) London, 1939.
Hollander, G. P., *Soviet Political Indoctrination*, New York, 1972.
Hookman, H., *History of China*, London, 1969.
Hottman, J., *Propaganda of Napoleon*, London, 1950.
Huizinga, J., *The Waning of the Middle Ages*, (transl.), London, 1955.
Innis, H. A., *Empire and Communications*, Toronto, 1952.
Kanet, R. E., *The Soviet Union and Developing Nations*, London, 1971.
Kantorowicz, E., *Frederick II*, London, 1957.
Kulstein, P., *Napoleon III and the Working Class*, Los Angeles, 1969.
Laprade, W. T., *Public Opinion and Politics in Eighteenth Century England*, New York, 1936.
Latey, M., *Tyranny*, London, 1972.
Laurence, J., *The Seeds of Disaster: South African Propaganda*, London, 1968.
Leith, J., *The Idea of Art as Propaganda in France, 1750-1799*, Toronto, 1965.
Mackenzie, A. J., *The Propaganda Boom*, London, 1938.
Morris, J., *Pax Britannica*, London, 1968.
Oldenbourg, Z., *The Crusades*, (transl.), London, 1966.
Palmer, R. R., *The Age of Democratic Revolution*, Princeton, 1959.
Perry, T. W., *Public Opinion, Propaganda and Politics in Eighteenth Century Britain*, London, 1961.
Robriquet, J., *Daily Life in the French Revolution*, (transl.), London, 1950.
Rudorff, R., *The Myth of France*, (transl.), London, 1965.
Runcieman, J. C. S., *History of the Crusades*, Cambridge, 1951-54.
Savenkov, A. A., *Lenin ob organizatorskom znacheni propagandistkiha*, Leningrad, 1971.
Schiller, H., *Mass Communication and American Empire*, New York, 1958.
Schlesinger, A. M., *Prelude to Independence*, New York, 1958.

Shirer, W., *The Rise and Fall of the Third Reich*, London, 1960.

Smith, A. C. H., *Paper Voices: The Popular Press in Social Change 1935-65*, London, 1969.

Sorenson, T. C., *The World War*, New York, 1968.

Spector, R., *The English Literary Periodical and the Climate of Opinion during the Seven Years War*, London, 1959.

Speer, A., *Inside the Third Reich*, (transl.), London, 1955.

Suetonius, *The Twelve Caesars*, (transl.), London, 1946.

Talbot-Rice, T., *Russian Art*, London, 1950.

Tawney, R. H., *Religion and the Rise of Capitalism*, London, 1955.

Thompson, J. M., *Napoleon*, London, 1952.

Thompson, J. M., *The French Revolution*, London, 1943.

Toynbee, A., *A Study in History*, London, 1946.

Trevor-Roper, H., *Princes and Artists*, London, 1976.

Ullmann, W., *History of Political Thought in the Middle Ages*, London, 1965.

Ullmann, W., *Principles of Government and Politics in the Middle Ages*, Cambridge, 1961.

Ulam, A., *Lenin*, London, 1959.

Voprosy, *Teorii i Praktiki massovych sredstv Propagandy*, Moscow, 1969.

Virgil, *The Aeneid*, (transl.), London, 1949.

Ward, J. T., *Chartism*, London, 1962.

Weakland, J. H., *The Thought of Mao Tse Tung*, Palao Alto, 1968.

Wiskemann, E., *Europe of the Dictators*, London, 1966.

Wilson, B., *Sects*, London, 1962.

White, T. H., *The Making of a President, 1960*, New York, 1961.

Woolf, S. J., *The Italian Risorgimento*, London, 1969.

Wykes, A., *The Nuremberg Rallies*, London, 1970.

Yu, F. T. C., *The Establishment of Propaganda Networks in China*, Dallas, 1952.

Zeman, Z. A. B., *Nazi Propaganda*, London, 1973.

INDEX

A.

Access to media, 36.
Acton, Lord, 29.
Adams, Samuel, 86.
Agitation, 7.
Ahja, 65.
Alexander the Great, 35, 49, 95.
Alliteration, 18, 58.
Andersen, Hans, 48.
Anthems, 11, 45.
Anti-Semitism, 69, 82, 102, 111.
Antony, Mark, 60.
Architecture, 41, 63, 68, 74, 78, 94, 96.
Argentine, 12, 119.
Arianism, 30.
Aristotle, 5, 48.
Athens, 56.
Auber, 45.
Audience research, 31.
Augustus, 60-65, 87.
Austria, 77, 116.

B.

Ballads, 13.
Banda, 20.
Bandwagon effect, 28.
Barclay, W., 65.
Barthes, R., 3.
Beethoven, 115.
Belder, E. A., 70.
Benn, A. Wedgewood. 51.
Bibaculus, 58.
Bismarck, 12, 102.
Blumler, J., 29.
Blyton, Enid, 48.
Boorstin, D. J., 22.
Booth, General, 127.
Boston Tea Party, 86.
Brainwashing, 7.
Bramante, 78.
Brant, Sebastian, 76.

Brawn, Max, 115.
Brazil, Angela, 49.
Brazil, 116.
Briggs, Asa, 50.
Britain, 125.
British Empire, 5, 101.
Brown, J. A. C., 151.
Buchan, J., 48.
Buddha, 9.
Bullock, A., 113.
Bunyan, J., 18, 78.
Burckhard, J., 48, 78.
Burgein, O., 23.
Burgh, 85.
Burgundy, Dukes of, 72.
Burke, J., 93.
Butler, Lady J., 43, 101.
Buttons, 40, 48.
Byron, Lord, 47, 99.

C.

Caesar, Julius, 5, 11, 37, 41, 49, 55-60.
Capa, Robert, 44.
Cards, 40, 89.
Caricature, 40.
Carnot, 98.
Castro, F., 20.
Catullus, 59.
Cavour, 100.
Cellular propaganda, 14, 65, 91, 104, 129.
Chadwick, 99.
Charlemagne, 20, 63.
Chartism, 98.
Chiang Ching, 122.
Chiang Kai Chek, 129.
China, 118, 129.
Chivalry, 34, 72.
Chotiner, Moray, 124.
Chow, Yung, 120.
Christian Science, 127.

Churchill, W., 20, 50.
Cicero, 53.
Cinema, 49, 102, 103, 111, 109, 115, 122.
Cleopatra, 58.
Cliché, 20, 23, 118.
Clodius, 57.
Cobden, J., 99.
Cohn, N., 21, 71.
Coins, 58.
Columbus, 47, 76.
Communism, 17, 38, 98, 104, 123.
Confucius, 119.
Conservation, 11.
Cox, D. F., 32.
Cranach, 77.
Cromwell, Oliver, 48, 79.
Crossman, R. H. S., 29.
Crowns, 11.
Crusades, 5, 38, 69-70.
Czechoslovakia, 44, 126.

D.
D'Annunzio, 47, 113.
Danton, 90.
David, 91, 111, 116.
Delacroix, 43, 120.
Demosthenes, 55.
De Saussure, F., 23.
Deviation, 30.
Dickens, A. G., 10, 75-76.
Dickens, C., 48.
Didactic propaganda, 12.
Diderot, 49, 88.
Dietrich, Otto, 113.
Disraeli, 101.
Doob, L. W., 16.
Dreyfus, 102.
Dumouriez, 92.
Durandus, W., 75.
Dürer, 42, 78.

E.
Eckart, 113.
Economic propaganda, 11.
Eddy, Mary B., 127.
Education, 30.
Egypt, 13.
Eisenhower, D. D., 124.

Eisenstein, S., 44, 115, 122.
Eleusis, 21.
Elgar, 101.
Emerson, 34.
Enthusiasm, 11, 27, 65.
Enzenburger, H. M., 29.
Ezekiel, 68.

F.
Fabergé, 38.
Fasces, 39, 116.
Festinger, L., 26.
Fichte, 100.
Figaro, 46.
Figurative language, 17.
Flagellants, 12.
Flags, 11, 88.
Foxe, 78.
France, 88-92.
Francis, 111.
Franklin, B., 26, 86, 87.
French Revolution, 10, 38, 88-92.
Frederick Barbarossa, 73.
Frederick of Bohemia, 81.
Frederick the Great, 49, 115.
Freud, S., 9.

G.
Gandhi, M., 20, 130.
Gans, H. J., 4, 7.
Gapon, Father, 106.
Garibaldi, 20, 100.
Gerasimov, 109.
Gerbner, 4.
Gericault, 93.
Germany, 100, 112-118.
Ghenghis Khan, 35.
Gladstone, W. E., 42.
Goebbels, 26, 112-118.
Goldsmith, 97.
Gollob, H. F., 32.
Gorky, M., 106.
Goya, 43.
Grant, M. J., 55.
Graphic media, 39, 68.
Greek religion, 42.
Gregory, I, 69.
Gregory VII, 70.
Grierson, J., 50.

Gros, 96.
Grote, 49.
Guevara, 20.
Gustavus Adolphus, 81.

H.
Haggard, R., 102.
Haw Haw, 12, 115.
Haydn, 45.
Hearst, R., 103.
Hebert, 92.
Henderson, W., 116.
Hendry, G. A., 48, 101.
Heraldry, 39.
History, 5, 11, 49.
Hitler, 5, 8, 20, 28, 37, 43, 49,
   87, 100, 110, 111-118.
Hitler Youth, 30, 111-118.
Hindenburg, 117.
Hobbes, 49.
Hoffer, E., 2.
Hogarth, 82.
Hoggart, R., 46.
Hohlwein, 116.
Hollywood, 49.
Horace, 47, 62.
Horne, 99.
Horst Wessell, 41, 111.
Hovland, C., 27.
Hugo, V., 97.
Huizinga, T., 72-74.
Huxley, A., 117.

I.
Imitation, 49.
Imperialism, 98, 100, 101, 129.
India, 101, 130.
Induced response, 27.
Inhibiting factors, 23.
Inflation, 11.
Initials, 39.
Intimidation, 27.
Isaiah, 65.
Islanm, 65.
Italy, 110.

J.
Jacobinism, 91-92.
Jacobitism, 45, 80.
Japanese, 22, 103, 128.
Jeaurat, 93.

Jefferson, T., 86, 87.
Jesuits, 40, 78, 129.
Jesus Christ, 19, 20, 37, 55, 64,
   67.
Joan of Arc, 74.
Joffe, 108.
John Bull, 19.
Jovis, D., 71.
Judaism, 13, 42.

K.
Kaiser, 12, 58.
Kamikazi, 22.
Kennedy, J., 20, 125.
Kenyatta, J., 20, 130.
Khachaturian, 109.
Kingsley, C., 48.
Kipling, R., 47, 101.
Klapper, J. T., 23.
Knox, R., 12.
Koestler, A., 25.
Komsomol, 30, 110.
Kruger, 11.
Kruschev, 109.

L.
Labour Party, 125.
Lasswell, H., 3, 5, 7, 29.
Le Brun, 88.
Lenin, 5, 7, 9, 14, 30, 66, 85,
   104-6.
Li Chi, 120.
Lillibullero, 45.
Lippmann, W., 23.
Liverpool, Lord, 56.
Li Tsing Tin, 119.
Livy, 63.
Locke, J., 49.
Lo Jui Ching, 120.
Loyola, 75-7.
Luegar, 113.
Lu Hsun, 121.
Luther, 9, 15, 47.

M.
Macarthy, J., 21, 71.
McLuhan, M., 3, 4, 14, 104.
MacQuail, D., 22, 29, 30.
Maecenas, 62.
Magic, 67.

Maguire, W. J., 25, 31.
Mao Tse Tung, 14, 17, 20, 119.
Marat, 8, 90.
Marianne, 19.
Marie Antoinette, 38, 91.
Marseillaise, 45.
Martyrdom, 20.
Marvel, A., 80.
Marx, K., 17, 25, 104.
Masaryk, 20, 50.
Mass observation, 24.
Matarazzo, 78.
Maximilian, 77.
Mazzini, 100.
Media, 15, 30.
Media research, 10.
Merkurov, 109.
Metaphor, 18, 19, 65, 68, 133, 130.
Methodism, 27, 84.
Middle Ages, 8.
Millennialism, 44, 104 .
Miller, G., 24.
Milton, J., 47, 79.
Mirabeau, 90.
Mohammed, 18, 20.
Mommsen, 49.
Monasticism, 38.
Money, 11.
More, Hannah, 46, 93.
Music, 44, 74, 94, 109, 114.
Mussolini, 49, 63, 113.
Mythology, 122.

N.

Napoleon, 5, 11, 22, 37, 49, 63, 95, 98.
Napoleon III, 41, 97.
Nationalism, 34, 96.
Necker, 88.
Nero, 56, 63.
New Testament, 8.
Nicholas, Tsar, 11, 38.
Nixon, R., 124.
Nordenstreng, K., 6.
Novel, 48.
Nuremberg, 116-117.

O.

O'Connor, 99.

Otto, James, 86.
Opera, 46, 80.
Oppius Gaius, 57.
Oratory, 44.
Owen, R., 21.

P.

Packard, V., 4, 124.
Paine, T., 15, 46, 82, 85, 86, 92.
Painting, 42, 88, 91, 93, 96, 100, 101, 109, 119.
Palmer, I. R. R., 92.
Parable, 65.
Paradox, 20.
Parody, 22.
Papacy, 37, 42, 68-74, 97.
Patriotism, 67.
Peng Chen, 120.
Pentecostalists, 124.
Perry, T. W. W., 82.
Personification, 19.
Peter the Hermit, 65, 69.
Photography, 44.
Pickles, W., 27.
Pilkington Report, 51.
Plekhanov, 107.
Polarisation, 29.
Pompey, 58.
Portugal, 110.
Posters, 80, 112, 116.
Price, Richard, 85.
Printing, 15, 47, 98.
Puns, 19.

R.

Radek, 107.
Radio, 49, 111, 114.
Rama Krishna, 128.
Reeves, R., 124.
Reformation, 5, 42.
Revere, Paul, 86.
Response analysis, 32.
Reuter, 37.
Rhyme, 17, 18.
Rhythm, 17, 18.
Riesman, M., 126.
Robespierre, 90.
Robinson, F., 127.
Roman Catholicism, 3.

Romans, 5, 8, 37, 55-64.
Roosevelt, F. D., 50.
Rousseau, J. J., 90.
Russian Revolution, 104-112.
Russell, C., 127.

S.

Saar, 115.
Sachs, H., 77.
St. Paul, 9, 27, 44, 67.
St. Peter, 65, 69.
St. Simeon Stylites, 35.
St. Simon, 100.
Sallust, 58.
Salvation Army, 127.
Sargant, W., 17, 57, 71, 78.
Schramm, W., 23, 30.
Scott, G. S., 101.
Sculpture, 41, 109.
Self denial, 67.
Sforza, 78.
Shaftesbury, 99.
Shakespeare, 48.
Shostakovich, 45, 109.
Sieyes, 88.
Socrates, 4.
Soka Gakkai, 128.
Solzhenitsyn, 110.
Song of Roland, 10.
Sources, 8.
Sparta, 22, 67.
Spectacle, 63, 68, 94, 116, 123.
Speer, A., 41, 112-118.
Stalin, 8, 41, 67, 110.
Stella, J., 81.
Streicher, J., 57.
Strive, 108.
Suetonius, 58.
Swastika, 41, 112, 116, 117.
Symbols, 42, 66, 68, 74, 88, 102,
    107, 123.
Syme, R., 62.

T.

Tanzania, 129.
Tawney, R. H., 35.
Television, 25, 36, 50, 51.
Teng To, 120.
Terrorisation, 7.
Theatre, 48, 94, 122.

Theophilus, 75.
Thyssen, 114.
Tibullus, 62.
Tilly, 19, 22, 81.
Tombs, 11.
Tory Party, 125.
Toynbee, A., 5.
Trappists, 35.
Triumphs, 11.
Trotsky, 20, 30.
Tsars, 58, 104.
Tucker, J., 83.
Tunstall, J., 37.
Tyrtaeus, 47.

U.

Ullman, W., 68, 70.
United Nations, 23.
United States, 1, 80.
Urban II, 71.

V.

Varro, T., 55.
Vikings, 22.
Virgil, 22, 47, 61, 63.
Virgin Mary, 42, 74.
Voltaire, 87.

W.

Walter Sans Devoir, 72.
War propaganda, 11.
Washington, G., 87.
Webb, P. W., 83.
Werner, 76.
Wesley, J., 27, 44, 46, 84.
Wessell, Horst, 20.
Wilde, Oscar, 58.
Wilhelm II, 100, 102.
Wilkes, J., 8, 82-83.
Williams, R., 6.
Wolfe, T., 92.
World War I, 101, 118.
World War II, 5.
Wren, P. C., 48.

X, Y, Z

Zimbardo, P. G., 27.
Zola, E., 48.
Zoroastrianism, 21.